OUT OF THE DEPTHS

out of

of

STUDIES INTO THE

MEANING OF THE

BOOK OF PSALMS

Bernhard W. Anderson

the

depths

Joint Commission on Education and Cultivation
Board of Missions, United Methodist Church
475 Riverside Drive
New York, N. Y. 10027

LIBRARY OF CONGRESS CATALOG CARD NO. 75-98112

COVER: Bert Waggott
FORMAT: Mamie Harmon

In Memory of My Mother

Grace Word Anderson

Psalm 23:4

CONTENTS

This is a study book on the Psalms of the Old Testament—written at the request of the Women's Division of the Board of Missions of The United Methodist Church. Given the purpose of the book, it is appropriate to indicate at the outset a few directions for study.

1. This study finds a way through the Psalter with the aid of the "form-critical" method advocated by two leading scholars of the twentieth century: Hermann Gunkel and Sigmund Mowinckel. Instead of tracing *themes* through the Psalter, we are going to study the Psalms according to *types* which can be classified on the basis of their literary form and situation in worship. It will be handy to refer from time to time to the appendices at the back of the book where the classification is conveniently given.

2. Since this is not intended as a book *about* the Psalms but a guide *into* the Psalms, it is extremely important that you read the psalms themselves carefully and devotionally, following the study plan as it unfolds, chapter by chapter. In each chapter groups of psalms are taken up according to their type and liturgical setting. If you cannot read all the psalms in these groups, read at least those recommended (marked with an asterisk) and, preferably, read them from *The Oxford Annotated Bible with the Apocrypha*, edited by Herbert G. May and Bruce M. Metzger (New York: Oxford, 1965). This ecumenical edition of the Bible, based on the Revised Standard Version, contains helpful notes to the Psalms and other aids.

3. The study is undertaken with the conviction that the Psalter is "The Prayer Book of the Bible" which contains prayers to be offered in the name of Jesus Christ. In each chapter I have lifted up some big theological

question (revelation in history, the enemies that threaten us, the power of death, the Name of God, the advent of God's kingdom, the problem of suffering) with which the church wrestles as it re-reads the Psalms in the situation in which it now finds itself in its ongoing historical pilgrimage. It is hoped that the study will lead to a deeper understanding of the place of the Psalter in the church's worship.

4. There are two paperbacks which I wish were in the possession of those who use this study book. One is *The Faith of the Psalmists* by Helmer Ringgren who has taught at Garrett Theological Seminary and is now professor in the University of Turku, Finland. The other is *Introduction to the Psalms* by Christoph Barth, a son of Karl Barth who has taught for a number of years in Indonesia at the Djakarta Theological Seminary and is now professor at the University of Mainz, Germany. Both of these scholars stand within the form-critical tradition of Gunkel and Mowinckel and have helped us to understand the Psalms in the church. Ringgren stresses the importance of the cult for the expression of piety; Barth tends to emphasize major theological issues which arise out of the context of worship. By means of footnotes, I have keyed in these paperbacks at various points in the study, as well as the contributions of other scholars whose works are also listed in the bibliography.

I express thanks to my B.D. student Wayne Richards for permission to use his "contemporary lament," to my graduate student David Frame for his careful checking of the manuscript, and to the women of the Board of Missions of The United Methodist Church for being patient with me when I was writing this study book in a difficult time. Special thanks go to three women in my life: first, to my wife who has gone through this study of the Psalms with me and has helped me more than I can say; second to my daughter, Carol Warthin, who has assisted in the preparation of the manuscript for publication; and, finally and especially, to my mother, whose life on earth came to fulfillment in the years 1946-1966 when she served the church as Director of Beulah Home in Oakland, California.

Bernhard W. Anderson

Princeton Theological Seminary
January 1, 1970

1:

THE PSALMS
AND THE
WORSHIPING COMMUNITY

In our troubled times the church is reliving the experience of the ancient Israelites after the exodus from Egypt, when the short route into the promised land was cut off and "God led the people around by the way of the wilderness" (Ex. 13:18). In their journey through history the People of God discover that the goal is not reached by the easy highway; instead, they must take the roundabout way, the detour into "the wasteland" (T. S. Eliot) which poets and artists have portrayed. Yet in this present time of the church's wandering in the wilderness something wonderful has happened: people have learned to praise God anew, and to praise him not just in the times of his presence but in the times of his absence. Even when called upon to undergo in loneliness the severest trials, separated from the visible support of the Christian fellowship, they have learned to sing songs of praise to God—especially the songs found in the book of Psalms. Just as early Christians sang songs of praise while in prison (Acts 16:25) or on the way to the arena, so in our turbulent period of history the witnesses of Jesus Christ have joined with the worldwide believing community in singing "psalms and hymns and spiritual songs" (Ephesians 5:19).

This was the experience of one German pastor—now a professor at the University of Heidelberg—in the time of the Second World War. During his imprisonment in a German prison camp, Claus Westermann had with him a copy of Luther's translation of the New Testament and the Psalms, and so he turned to the study of the Psalms according to Luther's free version. In a recent book he writes about what these songs meant to people in times of trial:[1]

> Whenever one in his enforced separation praised God in song or speech, or silence, he was conscious of himself not as an individual, but as a member of the congregation. When in hunger and cold, between interrogations, or as one sentenced to death, he was privileged to praise God, he knew that in all his ways he was borne up by the church's praise of God.

Others have testified that the Psalms have enabled them to speak to God "out of the depths" with the whole church of Jesus Christ. Dietrich Bonhoeffer, the martyred Christian whose writings have profoundly influenced contemporary theology, regarded the Psalter as his favorite book in the Bible. His last publication before his execution in the Nazi period was *The Prayer Book of the Bible: An Introduction to the Psalms* (1940). In this pamphlet he developed the view that just as Jesus Christ has taught us to pray the words of the Lord's Prayer, so "the prayer book of the Bible" contains in greater fulness and richness the words which God wants us to speak to him in the name of Jesus Christ. He argued that it is proper, therefore, for the New Testament and the Psalms to be bound together; for, as one of his interpreters, John Godsey, puts it, "it is the prayer of the church of Jesus Christ and belongs to the Lord's Prayer." [2]

New Songs

Gideons

The bracketing together of the New Testament and the Psalms, as in the case of the Lutheran edition just mentioned, points to the important place of the Psalms in Christian worship. As a matter of fact, the title "the book of Psalms" comes from the New Testament (Luke 20:42; Acts 1:20). In the Hebrew Bible the title is *Tehillim*, which means "songs of praise"; but the early Christian community read the Old Testament in the Greek version (Septuagint), where the prevailing title was *psalmoi*, referring to songs sung to the accompaniment of stringed instruments. One Codex of the Greek Old Testament used the title *psalterion*, a term which referred basically to a zither-like instrument and secondarily to songs with stringed accompaniment; hence the alternate title "Psalter." From the very first, Christians treasured "the book of Psalms" or "the Psalter" very highly. It is true that the early followers of Jesus of Nazareth expressed their faith in the singing of "a new song"; yet this "new speech from the depths," as Amos Wilder points out, drew deeply upon fountains that sprang up within worship.[3] The early church was profoundly influenced by synagogue worship in which psalms were read as scripture, recited as prayers, or sung as hymns.

Down through the Christian centuries the Psalms have enjoyed an indispensable place in the liturgical practice of the church. Today in Roman Catholic and Eastern Orthodox churches—especially where the ancient monastic usage is still preserved—the entire Psalter is recited once each week. In the Anglican church the Psalms are repeated once a month. And in other churches in the Protestant tradition the profound influence of the Psalter is evident in the responsive reading of selected psalms or in the singing of hymns influenced by psalms such as "All People That on Earth Do Dwell" ("Old Hundred"—Ps. 100) or "A Mighty Fortress Is Our God" (the great Reformation hymn—Ps. 46). Indeed, when one considers the enriching and invigorating influence which the Psalms have exerted upon preaching, worship, and devotional life, it is no exaggeration for Christoph Barth to say that "the renewal and reunion of the Church, for which we are hoping, cannot come about without the powerful assistance of the Psalms—without the support of their incomparable words, and above all of their imperishable message." [4]

Now, the early Christian church did not appropriate the Psalter of Israel because it lacked the inspiration for composing new hymns with a distinctive Christian accent. Students of the New Testament are becoming increasingly aware of hymnic fragments and other liturgical materials now embedded in early Christian literature. For instance, in the magnificent portrayal of the humility of the Christ "who, though he was in the form of God, did not count equality with God a thing to be grasped, but emptied himself, taking the form of a servant" (Phil. 2:5-11), Paul clearly made use of an early Christian song that was familiar to his readers. Fragments of Christian hymnody are contained in the "new song" of Revelation 7:9-14, which Handel transposed into the triumphal music of *The Messiah* ("Worthy is the Lamb who was slain . . ."). And the Gospel of Luke includes two complete Christian psalms: the Magnificat of Mary (Luke 1:46-55) and the Benedictus of Zechariah (Luke 1:68-79). The Benedictus begins this way:

> *"Blessed be the Lord God of Israel,*
> *for he has visited and redeemed his people,*
> *and has raised up a horn of salvation for us*
> *in the house of his servant David,*
> *as he spoke by the mouth of his holy prophets*
> *from of old*
> *that we should be saved from our enemies,*

> *and from the hand of all who hate us;*
> *to perform the mercy promised to our fathers,*
> *and to remember his holy covenant, . . ."*

Here the language echoes that of the Psalms, including the mention of deliverance from enemies; but this is a *new song*, pitched in the brilliant key of the good news that in Jesus Christ God "has visited and redeemed his people."

What has happened in the New Testament is that the Christian community has appropriated the whole body of Jewish scriptures—in Christian terms known as "the Old Testament"—and, in so doing, has "baptized the Psalter into Christ." [5] Along with the prophecy of Isaiah, the Psalter is one of the two Old Testament books most frequently drawn upon in the New Testament. Early Christians, who regularly used the book of Psalms in worship, wanted to say that these songs bear witness to Jesus Christ. Thus the royal psalm, Psalm 2, with its divine declaration "Thou art my Son," was understood to refer to *the* Anointed One (Messiah), Jesus Christ; and Psalm 22, a song of lament beginning with a poignant cry of dereliction, "My God, why hast thou forsaken me?" was taken to be a portrayal of Christ's passion. In saying that these and other psalms refer to Christ, the church's intention was to identify itself with the community of Israel which God had called into his service. The church confessed that the Old Testament, Christianly speaking, was indeed part of "the story of our life," a story of God's action with his people Israel which leads to and is illumined by God's visitation in the historical event of Jesus Christ. From this perspective it may be said that the entire Psalter—and not just selected psalms which are interpreted "christologically" in the New Testament—is illumined by God's revelation

B. Graham

handwritten note: 23rd Psalm

in Jesus Christ. The whole Psalter is to be interpreted and prayed in the light of God's revelation in Christ.

PSALMS OF THE PILGRIM CHURCH

Our discussion of the church's role in composing and interpreting psalms leads to a very important point. The Psalms of the Bible are not individualistic poems such as a modern person might compose to express his own thoughts and feelings. Of course, according to the Bible the individual is infinitely important in God's sight. A psalmist, looking up at the starry skies, marvels that the God who holds the cosmos within his creative grasp actually visits and cares for man and, moreover, invests him with the noble responsibility of being his representative who exercises dominion over the earth (Ps. 8:3-8). Yet the individual *finds himself* in the community which God has called into being. Within that community he has access to God in worship; he joins with the community in responding in praise to God's actions; and he participates in the great historical pilgrimage of the People of God. As we are reminded by the Vatican II documents dealing with the nature of the church, the Bible is the story of "God's pilgrim people."

It should not be surprising, then, to discover that the songs of this pilgrim people are not confined to the Psalter but are found in connection with the whole unfolding story—not only in the New Testament, as we have noticed, but throughout the Old Testament. More and more we are coming to learn that many of the materials in the Old Testament, such as the story of creation in Gen. 1:1-2, 4a, were shaped by liturgical usage, perhaps in connection with one of the great temple festivals. In addition, numerous psalms are scattered throughout the Old Testament. As a preface to our concentrated study of the book of Psalms, it would be helpful to glance over some of these Old Testament psalms. The list includes:

1. The Song of the Sea (Ex. 15:1-18), composed to celebrate Yahweh's (RSV "the Lord's") deliverance of his people from Egyptian bondage. (Based on the "Song of Miriam," Ex. 15:20-21.)

2. The Song of Moses (Deut. 32:1-43), a song which contrasts God's faithfulness with Israel's unfaithfulness.

3. The Song of Deborah (Judges 5:1-31), a victory song composed to celebrate Yahweh's coming to the rescue of his embattled people.

4. The Song of Hannah (I Sam. 2:1-10), a psalm of thanksgiving inserted into the story about Samuel at Shiloh.

5. David's Song of Deliverance (II Sam. 22:2-51), a psalm of thanksgiving, preserved also as Psalm 18.

6. A song of thanksgiving (Isa. 12:4-6) used to conclude the first section of the book of Isaiah.

7. King Hezekiah's song (Isa. 38:9-20), a psalm of thanksgiving for use when presenting a thank-offering in the Temple.

8. The prayer of Habakkuk (Hab. 3:2-19), a hymn praising Yahweh for his victory on behalf of his people.

9. Jonah's prayer from the belly of a fish (Jonah 2:1-9), actually a psalm of thanksgiving.

10. Hymns embedded in the prophecy of Second Isaiah (e.g., 42:10-12; 52:9-10) which summon the earth to sing a "new song."

11. In the book of Job there are both hymns (e.g., 5:8-16; 9:4-10; 12:7-10; 12:13-25) and laments

(e.g., 3:3-12, 13-19, 20-26; 7:1-10; 7:12-21; 9:25-31; 10:1-22).

12. Psalms of lament are also found in the book of Jeremiah (e.g., 15:15-18; 17:14-18; 18:19-23) and in the book of Lamentations, especially chapters 3 and 5.

If one were to consider literature belonging to the Old Testament in expanded form (i.e., including the books often called the Apocrypha), it would be necessary to add other psalms to the list. For instance in Ecclesiasticus (otherwise known as the Wisdom of Jesus the son of Sirach) we find the thanksgiving of Sirach (51:1-12) and superb hymns of praise (39:14b-35; 42:15 to 43:33). And though we cannot go into all the relevant literature outside the scope of the Old Testament, special mention should also be made of the beautiful songs found among the Dead Sea Scrolls, apparently composed by members of the Qumran monastery for use in their worship services. In accordance with liturgical styles in vogue in the synagogue, these hymns fall into two main categories: thanksgivings ("I give thee thanks, O Lord . . .") and blessings ("Blessed art thou, O Lord . . .").[6]

Even this cursory review shows that the psalms preserved in the Psalter represent only a small selection of the many psalms which once were composed and sung in Israel. For the Bible as a whole is not only the story of God's dealings with his people but also the witness of his people's response in thanksgiving and adoration, in lament and petition along the way of its pilgrimage through history. The sounds of Israel's praises are heard, to one degree or another, in practically every book of the Bible, from Genesis to the Revelation of John. It is in the Psalter, however, that the praises of God's people resound clearly as nowhere else.

On first glancing through the Psalter we discover that the 150 psalms are arranged into five parts or "books." The structure of this song book is as follows:

Book   I: Psalms 1-41
              Concluding doxology: Ps. 41:13
Book   II: Psalms 42-72
              Concluding doxology: Ps. 72:18-19
Book III: Psalms 73-89
              Concluding doxology: Ps. 89:52
Book IV: Psalms 90-106
              Concluding doxology: Ps. 106:48
Book   V: Psalms 107-150
              Concluding doxology for the whole
              Psalter: Ps. 150

Notice that each of the first four books concludes with a brief doxology which is not a literary part of the psalm with which it is associated. Psalm 150 not only fittingly concludes the last book but rounds off the entire Psalter with a doxology.

Just as the Psalter appropriately ends with an invocation to praise, so it suitably begins by striking the keynotes of Israel's faith. It is not accidental that the Psalter in its present form opens with two key psalms: Psalm 1, which extols the virtue of meditating on the Law (Torah); and Psalm 2, which was regarded in the late Old Testament period as referring to the Messiah (literally, "the Anointed One"). These two themes—the revelation of God's will in the Torah and the belief in the coming of the Messiah to inaugurate God's kingdom —constituted the two cardinal beliefs of the Jewish people at the time the Psalter was given its final form.

This five-fold arrangement of the Psalter was made relatively late in the Old Testament period and was undoubtedly patterned after the Torah (Pentateuch) which was divided into five books (Genesis through Deuteronomy). In its present form the Psalter comes from the period of the Second Temple—the temple of Zerubbabel which was rebuilt in 520-515 B.C. (the time of the prophets Haggai and Zechariah) and stood until it was superseded by the temple of King Herod (begun about 20 B.C.), the stones of which may still be seen in the famous "Wailing Wall" of Jerusalem. Sometimes the Psalter is spoken of as "the hymnbook of the Second Temple." This is proper insofar as the Psalter was given its final shape and was used in temple services during this period. Yet this was also the period when the synagogue was emerging as the focal point of prayer and interpretation of scripture. Therefore the Psalter may be called the prayer book of the synagogue with equal justification, especially since it opens with a psalm praising the Torah.

As a matter of historical fact, the rise of the synagogue was a major factor in keeping alive the faith and tradition of Israel in a time when Jewish colonies were springing up outside of Palestine. Alexandria in Egypt came to be one of the major centers of the Jewish "dispersion" in the postexilic period. About 250 B.C. the Alexandrian Jews began to translate their sacred scriptures into the vernacular—which for them was the ordinary Greek of the Hellenistic world. This Greek version of the Old Testament (known as the Septuagint) contains a Psalter which differs in several interesting respects from the Hebrew tradition followed by the Protestant Reformers. For one thing, the Greek Old Testament—like the scriptures of the Dead Sea community of Qumran—contains an extra psalm (Psalm 151)[7] which is attributed to David. The Greek Bible also differs somewhat in the determination of where a particular psalm begins and ends; for instance, what is regarded as one psalm in the Greek version may appear as two in the Hebrew Bible (e.g., Pss. 9-10). Since the early Christian church read its Old Testament in Greek, this structure of the Psalter has profoundly influenced Christian usage, as may be seen by consulting the translations used in the Roman Catholic and Eastern Orthodox church. In this study, however, we shall follow the numbering of the Revised Standard Version, which is that of the Hebrew Bible, and retain the Name *Yahweh* (translated, "the Lord," in the Revised Standard Version).

This numbering will have to be reconsidered at points for, as we shall see, some psalms considered as two in the Hebrew Bible are actually one (e.g., Ps. 42-43), and vice versa, a psalm which is considered as one may be two (e.g., Ps. 27). In other words the numerical determination of the psalms does not always coincide with the literary units. (See Appendix B.)

A closer look at the five-fold structure of the Hebrew Psalter reveals that this symmetrical organization was superimposed upon previously circulating collections of psalms, just as a modern hymnbook is based upon previous editions of hymns of worship. Evidence of this is found in the editorial notice at the end of Psalm 72: "The prayers of David, the son of Jesse, are ended" (Ps. 72:20). This postscript is rather surprising when one discovers that psalms of David are found later on: Psalms 108-110, and Psalms 138-145, according to their headings. This can only mean that at one stage in the history of the formation of the Psalter a Davidic collection ended at this point.

Now, when we look at the psalms up to this point (Pss. 3-72; minus Pss. 1 and 2 which are introductory to the whole Psalter), we find that there are actually two groups of psalms which, by their headings, are ascribed to David: namely, Psalms 3-41 [8] and Psalms 51-72. In between these two Davidic collections we find a group of Psalms ascribed to Korah (Pss. 42-49); and just after the second Davidic collection we find another group ascribed to Asaph (Pss. 73-83). We gather from the Book of Chronicles (written about 300 B.C.) that Korah and Asaph were leaders of musical guilds during the period of the Second Temple (see, e.g., II Chron. 20:19). It seems likely, then, that the original nucleus of the Psalter was the Davidic collection found in Psalms 3-41. In the course of time this collection was supplemented with other Davidic collections (especially Pss. 51-72), and with various collections composed and used by the choirs of the Second Temple (Pss. 42-49, 73-83, 84-89). Eventually the collections now found in Psalms 90-150 were added. In this last section of the Psalter we find, for instance, a group of psalms which celebrate Yahweh's kingship over the earth (Pss. 93-99). Another group is characterized by the exclamation "Praise Yahweh," which in Hebrew is *hallelujah* (Pss. 111-113, 115-117, 135, 146-150). And still another group bears the superscription "Song of Ascents" (Pss. 120-134), an expression which probably means "a pilgrimage song," that is, a song used when pilgrims ascended to Jerusalem to worship at the Temple. Psalm 122, for instance, expresses the pilgrim's joy on having arrived at his destination.

I was glad when they said to me,
    "Let us go to the house of Yahweh!"
Our feet have been standing
    within your gates, O Jerusalem!
                —Psalm 122:1-2

In summary, we find embedded within the present edition of the Psalter the following collections:

1. An original Davidic collection (Pss. 3-41)
2. Psalms of the Korah musical guild (Pss. 42-49)
3. A second Davidic collection (Pss. 51-72)
4. Psalms of the Asaph musical guild
   (Pss. 73-83 + Ps. 50)
5. Additional psalms of musical guilds (Pss. 84-89)
6. Various other collections (Pss. 90-150), including
   (a) Psalms of Yahweh's kingship (Pss. 93-99)
   (b) Psalms of pilgrimage (Pss. 120-134)
   (c) Hallelujah psalms (Pss. 104-106, 111-113, 135, 146-150)

The collections shown with a bracket in the above outline (Nos. 2, 3, 4)—the so-called Elohistic Psalter—at one time circulated as a separate hymnbook. This is evident only from the text of the original Hebrew Bible, in which all these psalms show a decided preference to use the general name "God" (Elohim) instead of the special divine name, Yahweh (RSV "the Lord").* Some statistician has computed that in this "Elohistic Psalter" (Pss. 42-83) the divine name Elohim appears 200 times and Yahweh only 43, whereas in the rest of the Psalter Yahweh appears 642 times and Elohim only 29. The best explanation for this striking phenomenon is that this collection once existed independently before it was included in the final framework of the Psalter. This would explain why two psalms appear in almost identical form: Psalm 14 which uses the name Yahweh, and Psalm 53 which uses Elohim.

It is appropriate, then, to speak of the Psalter as "the hymnbook of the Second Temple" if we keep in mind that, like a modern church hymnal, it is a relatively late arrangement based on previous collections and including hymns of many ages. This is true, for instance, of the latest edition of *The Methodist Hymnal*. It includes

* See the Glossary under "Yahweh."

hymns from the Patristic period ("O Guide to Every Child" by Clement of Alexandria), from the Middle Ages ("Creator of the Stars of Night"—anonymous), from the Reformation (Luther's "A Mighty Fortress Is Our God"), from the period of the Enlightenment (Addison's "The Spacious Firmament"), from the great Wesleyan revival ("O For a Thousand Tongues to Sing"), to say nothing of modern hymns which reflect the pietism of the nineteeth century or the theological renaissance of the mid-twentieth century. Similarly, the Psalter, though it received its final form three or four centuries before Christ, reflects a long history of worship, reaching back at least to the time of David and, in some instances, including forms of worship used by Israel in the early period of the settlement in the land of Canaan. It covers almost 1000 years of the history of worship.

THE AUTHORSHIP OF THE PSALMS

In another respect, however, the comparison of the Psalter with a modern hymnbook does not hold. Most of the hymns in our hymnbooks are assigned to definite authors, whose dates are usually given in connection with the hymn. Relatively few modern hymns are anonymous; indeed, numerous books have been written about the authors of our great hymns. In the Psalter, however, the situation is just the opposite. The authors of the psalms are anonymous, and practically nothing can be learned from the psalms about the time or circumstance of their composition.

This statement may sound surprising in view of the traditional view that the book of Psalms contains the very words of David. Since the beginning of the Christian era, and indeed right to the nineteenth century, David has been regarded as the author of the Psalter. This view is reflected, for instance, in Mark 12:35-37 which reports Jesus' dispute with the scribes over the lineage and identity of the Messiah. The argument assumed that "David himself, inspired by the Holy Spirit," wrote Psalm 2, although in the Psalter this psalm, unlike many others, does not have a heading which attributes it to David. Jesus' argument, however, was *ad hominem*, that is, it was addressed to the prejudice of the scribes and was not intended to be a critical discussion of the authorship of the psalm. When it is assumed elsewhere in the New Testament that the Psalter is Davidic (e.g., Acts 4:25-26; Rom. 4:6-8), the writers merely adopted the contemporary way of referring to the hymnbook of Israel. In the same manner people of the time identified the Torah (Pentateuch) with Moses or Wisdom Literature with Solomon.

Even on critical grounds, however, the association of David with the Psalter is substantially valid. There was an ancient tradition, to which the prophet Amos appealed in the eighth century B.C. (Amos 6:5), that David was skillful with the lyre. It was this skill that brought him into the court of King Saul, according to a well-known story (I Sam. 16:14-23). Moreover, David gave great impetus to Israel's worship by bringing the Ark of the Covenant to Jerusalem (II Sam. 6) and by laying plans for the building of the Jerusalem Temple (II Sam. 7). Further, there must be considerable truth in the view expressed in the relatively late Chronicler's History that David sponsored the composition of psalms and was active in organizing the music and liturgy of Israel's worship (I Chron. 13-29). In the light of all this it may be assumed that imbedded in the Psalter are poems or poetic fragments actually composed by David or by those in his court. An example is Psalm 24, especially its concluding portion (vss. 7-10) with its address to the gates of Jerusalem to lift up their heads so that the

"King of glory" may enter—a ritual which clearly recalls David's bringing the Ark into his new capital.

Not all the Psalms, however, are attributed to David. The Psalter contains psalms attributed to the choir leader Asaph (12 psalms), to the Sons of Korah (11), to Moses (1 [Ps. 90]), to Solomon (2 [Pss. 72 and 127]), to Heman (1) and Ethan (1). Moreover, in the Hebrew Bible thirty-four psalms have no title at all, and for that reason they are known as "orphans." In all, seventy-three psalms bear the title *leDawid*, translated in the Revised Standard Version as "of David." Unfortunately, it is not clear what the preposition *le* means in this combination. It could mean "for David" or "concerning David," in which case one would think of a poem dedicated to the great king. David was "the favorite of the songs of Israel," to quote the RSV marginal translation at II Samuel 23:1 rather than the adopted translation "the sweet psalmist of Israel." On this view the psalms are Davidic in the sense that David was the favorite figure in the minds of composers, or perhaps they were composed at his orders or under his sponsorship. It may well be that in the earliest period of the collection of the Psalms the superscription *leDawid* designated psalms that were used in the royal (Davidic) cult, specifically "those psalms which the king was authorized to recite in the festival cult of the Temple." [9]

It is quite clear, however, that eventually the superscription *leDawid* was taken to mean "belonging to David" in the sense that the songs in question were composed by David. Clearly this view was held at the time thirteen of these psalms (Pss. 3, 7, 18, 34, 51, 52, 54, 56, 57, 59, 60, 63, 142) were introduced with notes indicating when David supposedly composed or recited the psalm. A good example is the well-known penitential Psalm 51 which bears this superscription: "A psalm of David, when Nathan the prophet came to him, after he had gone in to Bathsheba" (cf., II Sam. 12). Since the conclusion contains a prayer for rebuilding the walls of Jerusalem (51:18-19), the psalm in its present form must come from a time much later than David. In the late Old Testament period there was a tendency to ascribe more and more psalms to situations in David's life; and eventually, as we have seen, the whole Psalter was associated with the great name of David. For Israel, this ascription did not necessarily indicate authorship; rather, it signified that the community identified itself with David as it came before God in worship. David was an archetypal figure whose career portrayed both the misery and grandeur of the People of God. Therefore, as Christoph Barth points out, the people remembered "the king, pursued and abandoned in innocence and guilt, but always delivered and restored to power by the faithfulness of God, in whom their own existence as the People of God had found an expression that was valid for all time." [10] In a troubled time when Israel had no king, the people found in the story of David not only the archetype of its own existence but also the prototype of the coming King who would inaugurate God's kingdom.

THE SETTING OF THE PSALMS IN WORSHIP

The question of the authorship of the psalms fades into insignificance before the larger question of the "cultic" use of psalms, that is, their place and function in worship. A small clue to the cultic use of the Psalms is found in the enigmatic word *selah* which appears here and there (Pss. 3:2, 8; 9:16, 20, etc.). Possibly the term indicated a break or interlude in the recitation of the psalm, at which time the choir or instrumental accompanists would provide an intermezzo. In any case, the psalms were intended to be sung. This is evidenced by other musical notations, such as the instructions found at the head of Psalm 22: "To the choirmaster: according to The Hind of the Dawn." The curious words "The Hind of the Dawn" may refer to the tune to which the psalm was to be sung. The various directions on how the psalms were to be sung were added later, of course, but they emphasize the place of the Psalms in the setting of worship.

This brings us to an important point. The main question to ask about any psalm is not the situation in the life of David or in the life of some unknown individual which occasioned the composition. Nor is it essential to try to discover the historical situation in the life of the people Israel in which the psalm was composed, for with the exception of Psalm 137, which clearly presupposes life in Babylonian exile, there are very few historical hints for dating individual psalms. Rather the important question is the purpose of the psalm, and usually this question leads to an inquiry into the psalm's *situation in worship*. To be sure, not every psalm was composed for use in public worship. Psalm 45, for instance, is a secular ode intended for a royal wedding. But by and large the Psalms belong within the setting of Israel's worship. The psalmists blend their voices in the chorus of the People of God who respond to God's presence or his absence in their ongoing historical pilgrimage. Therefore the psalms in which *Israel* speaks to God are also intended *for us* who find ourselves caught up in the dramatic story of God's people.

In recent decades the approach to the Psalms in terms of their function and setting in worship has led to an exciting rediscovery of their meaning. The major pioneers in this rediscovery have been the German scholar Hermann Gunkel and the Scandinavian scholar Sigmund Mowinckel.[11] In this approach, which will be followed in the ensuing chapters of this study, there are two fundamental interests. First, psalms are classified according to literary type or genre. For instance, is a particular psalm a hymn intended to praise God for who he is and what he has done? Or is it a lament in which a suppliant cries to God for deliverance? And secondly, psalms are considered in terms of their setting in the worship of the People of God. Thus the *form* in which a psalm is cast is related to the *situation* in which it functions. Again the analogy to a modern church hymnbook may be helpful. Songs in a hymnal may be classified according to type (e.g., songs of adoration, of penitence, of thanksgiving, of trust), and also according to their place in a worship service or their use during one of the festivals of the church year (e.g., Christmas, Easter, Pentecost).

This "form-critical" approach to the Psalter, though it minimizes the importance of questions concerning the exact date and circumstances of the composition of a psalm, has helped to bring about a great reversal of judgment about the age of the Psalms as a whole. It was not many years ago that scholars, having abandoned the Davidic authorship of the Psalter, were saying that the vast majority of the Psalms are very late: postexilic, if not Maccabean. Today, however, many scholars insist that there are very few psalms that come from the postexilic period, the period of the Second Temple. Although the Psalter received its final form in that late period, the Psalms, for the most part, were used originally in the temple services during the preexilic period (from David to the fall of the First Temple: 1000 to 587 B.C.).

THE PSALMS AS PRAYED POETRY

Before turning attention to the Psalms according to their literary type and liturgical setting a special word should be said about the poetry of the Psalms. Considering that the Psalms were intended to be recited and sung to musical accompaniment, it is not surprising that they are cast in a poetic form whose exalted style, rhythmic cadences, interplay of imagery, and overtones of thought and feeling come through to the sensitive reader even in English translation. In ancient Israel the rhythm of worship not only involved poetic expression but bodily movement, as in the case of Miriam who "with timbrels and dancing" sang to Yahweh (Ex. 15:20-21) or David who with "all the house of Israel" danced and sang to the accompaniment of musical instruments as the Ark was escorted to Jerusalem (II Sam. 6:5). Contemporary expressions of worship in the form of the dance, perhaps to the accompaniment of a guitar, are quite in harmony with the worship presupposed in the Psalms!

The rhythm of worship is evident in the poetic structure of a psalm. Unlike our hymnody, Hebrew poetry is not governed by a sense of rhyme. Moreover, there is no consistent attempt to arrange every psalm into carefully measured stanzas, though sometimes a psalm is divided by recurring refrains (e.g., 46:7, 11; 80:3, 7, 19). Hebrew poetry has meter, to be sure, but the primary characteristic is "a rhythm of sense," as it has been called. The poetry is structured according to "poetic parallelism," that is, the first line is balanced by a corresponding line. The second line illuminates the first, and it does this in one of several ways:

    (a) sometimes the second line echoes the same theme in slightly different language—

The earth is the Lord's and the fulness thereof,
    the world and those who dwell therein.
                —Psalm 24:1

    (b) or the second line strengthens an affirmation by contrasting it with the opposite—

for the Lord knows the way of the righteous,
    but the way of the wicked will perish.
                —Psalm 1:6

(c) or the second line continues the thought, by ascending toward its completion—

For the Lord is a great God,
    and a great King above all Gods.
                  —Psalm 95:3

Examination of the poetry of the Psalms in terms of style, however, could lead no further than the conclusion that Israel shared patterns of form and style with her neighbors in the ancient Near East. Archaeological research has shown how heavily indebted Israel was to the surrounding culture, especially to the Canaanites whose poetic style and imagery are evident in many psalms (e.g., Pss. 18, 29, 68). However, the poetry of the Psalms is distinctive because it is "prayed poetry" (Westermann), that is, it is the language which the worshiping community uses to speak to God and about God, in response to his overtures in history.

Therefore it is important to give attention not only to the rhythms and forms of speech but to the language of metaphor. The psalmist uses language symbolically to express the depth dimension of human existence in all its joy and agony, its splendor and misery. He is not concerned to tell us about the details of his life or to disclose his own inner experiences. As an individual he recedes into anonymity; often he uses conventional imagery received from tradition. The psalmist's intention, however, is not to speak impersonally but to let the meaning of human existence vis-à-vis God burst forth with creative power through the poetic forms. Language is used poetically in order to portray experiences which are typical of all men, despite the variations which are as many as there are human beings. It is no wonder, then, that down through the centuries Christians have made the words of the Psalms their own. Because the psalmist speaks as a poet he also speaks to us and for us. He expresses the cry of every man "out of the depths."

2:

ENTHRONED
ON THE
PRAISES OF ISRAEL

The Psalms, as we have seen, are the songs which accompany the People of God on their journey through history. In the Hebrew language these songs are called *tehillim*, "songs of praise." Strictly speaking, this title should be reserved for the type of psalm labeled the "hymn" (to be considered in chap. 5). Indeed, the one time the title occurs in the superscriptions to the Psalms it is applied to a hymnic form (Ps. 145). Yet in a larger sense it is appropriate that the title "songs of praise" was finally applied to the Psalter as a whole, which includes a variety of types of psalms: hymns, laments, thanksgivings, songs of trust, wisdom meditations, and others. For the truth is that every psalm, whatever its literary type and whatever its relation to the cult, is actually a song which extols and glorifies God. In one of the most poignant laments of the Psalter, Psalm 22, the psalmist affirms that Yahweh is "enthroned on the praises of Israel" (vs. 3).

Before considering the major types of psalms it is necessary, then, to inquire into the *basis* of Israel's worship. True, the Psalms are the responses of the worshiping community to the initiative of God. Israel's praise is a reflex of the prior action of God which moves his people to "seek his face" (Ps. 27:8). At the beginning of his *Confessions*, Augustine strikes this biblical note of the priority of God's action:

Thou movest us to delight in praising Thee; for Thou hast formed us for Thyself, and our hearts are restless till they find rest in Thee.[1]

But the question is: How is God's initiative manifested? What kind of experience awakens the impulse to praise?

INFLUENCES FROM ISRAEL'S ENVIRONMENT

This question about the basis of Israel's worship has received considerable attention in recent decades. Thanks to the light cast by archaeology upon the culture of the ancient Near East, we have become increasingly aware of Israel's profound indebtedness to the ritual and mythology of her neighbors. When the Israelites settled in the land of Canaan during the two centuries before David (ca. 1200-1000 B.C.), they became part of a world where forms of worship were already firmly established. This was true especially at places like Shechem, Bethel, and Jerusalem which had been Canaanite sanctuaries for centuries before they were taken over by Israel and converted to the worship of Yahweh. Beth-el literally means "house of El." El was the high god of the Canaanite pantheon, the "Father" of the gods, and the "Creator of creatures," as we know from mythological tablets found on the coast of Syria at Ras Shamra (ancient Ugarit), dating from about 1400 B.C.

Israel did not say a flat No of repudiation to the advanced culture into which she entered but rather said No and Yes. Faith in Yahweh, the God of Israel, demanded turning from other "gods" and, consequently, repudiating the theological presuppositions of the religions of the environment. These religions, with their elaborate myth and ritual, enabled men to find meaning and security within the natural order which moves serenely in the rhythms of seedtime and harvest, summer and winter, life and death. The modern counterpart would be a religion which diverts people from the conflicts and terrors of history and promises the peace which comes with integration into the status quo, "things as they are." Israel's faith, however, perceived divine reality in the dynamic arena of social change; hence, the first response to the religions of the environment was negative. There could be no compromise between faith in Yahweh and the gods of paganism. However, Israel's No at this deepest level was often accompanied by a Yes of appropriation, that is, by taking over forms of worship (such as sacrifice) and literary forms (such as the psalm) and converting them to the service of Yahweh. The three great agricultural festivals of the Canaanites were adopted, and eventually were adapted to decisive events in Israel's historical experience. "Three times in the year you shall keep a feast to me," was the command from Yahweh in Ex. 23:14, and as the context shows, these were the festival times of the Canaanite agricultural calendar (on the festivals, see chap. 6).

The situation Israel faced in Canaan was like many situations faced by the church as it has moved into alien cultures and has had to decide whether to adopt native forms of religious expression. This problem was vividly illustrated some years ago, when the author was teaching for a summer in a theological institute held in Ghana. A heated discussion arose as to whether the Christian churches should admit into their worship the rhythms of African drums and folk dances that were part of the native religion and communal life of the people. Some of the older generation (under the influence of the first missionary churches) opposed this radical step, knowing that the African drum "talks" its own languages (war, sex, native religion, etc.). Members of the younger generation, however, believed that the risks of using the drum and dance in worship were worth taking for the sake of letting the Christian faith become indigenous. Thus, in ever new ways the People of God have had to face the problem of re-expressing faith in the forms provided by different cultures.

This problem became crucial in the Old Testament period when Israelite leaders made the fateful decision to ask for a king to rule them "like all the nations" (I Sam. 8:4-22). The step was risky, as the prophet Samuel pointed out, for concentration of power in a king would deprive the people of their cherished liberties. But there was also a theological danger for, as recent studies in the "sacral kingship" of the ancient Near East have shown, the king was regarded as a being endowed with divine talents and enjoying a special relationship with the deity. To adopt kingship, then, was not only to run a political danger; it was to take the chance that "court poetry" of the ancient world would undermine the Israelite faith in Yahweh which received its classical and most vigorous expression in the time when Israel had no king. Liberal elements, however, insisted that Yahweh was leading his people forward into the new way of life and thought represented by the kingship (see chap. 6). Thus, the kingdom established by David and consolidated by his son Solomon was characterized by a new openness to cultural influences from Egypt, Mesopotamia, and elsewhere.

Therefore the psalms which were used in the worship services of the Jerusalem temple should be viewed in the wider context of the psalm literature of the ancient Near East: the Sumerians, Babylonians, Canaanites, and Egyptians. The psalms in Israel's Psalter are similar in form, and often in content, to the hymns and laments composed by Israel's neighbors. As an example we may take the following passage from a hymn to the Moon-God, *Sin*, which archaeologists found at the site of Nineveh, an ancient capital of the Assyrian empire. In its present form it dates from about the time of Jeremiah (seventh century B.C.), but the tablet states that it was copied from an older edition.

> O Lord, decider of the destinies of heaven and earth,
>   whose word no one alters,
> Who controls water and fire, leader of living creatures,
>   what god is like thee?
> In heaven who is exalted? Thou! Thou alone art
>   exalted.
> On earth who is exalted? Thou! Thou alone art ex-
>   alted.
> Thou! When thy word is pronounced in heaven the
>   Igigi prostrate themselves.
> Thou! When thy word is pronounced on earth the
>   Anunnaki kiss the ground.
> Thou! When thy word drifts along in heaven like the
>   wind it makes rich the feeding and drinking of
>   the land.
> Thou! When thy word settles down on the earth green
>   vegetation is produced.
> Thou! Thy word makes fat the sheepfold and the
>   stall; it makes living creatures widespread.
> Thou! Thy word causes truth and justice to be, so that
>   the people speak the truth.
> Thou! Thy word which is far away in heaven, which
>   is hidden in the earth is something no one sees.
> Thou! Who can comprehend thy word, who can equal
>   it?
> O Lord, in heaven as to dominion, on earth as to valor,
>   among the gods thy brothers, thou hast not a
>   rival.[2]

Compare the language of this hymn with passages from Israel's psalms which raise the question: "Who is like thee, O Yahweh, among the gods?" (Ex. 15:11; Ps. 86: 8-10; and especially Ps. 89:5-14).

We may take a step further. Not only are there striking formal similarities to the songs of Israel's neighbors but in a few instances Israel has taken over hymns from the Canaanite environment (just as the church has borrowed pagan or "secular" melodies and poetry), and used them in the praise of Yahweh. One example is Psalm 29 which is an adaptation of a Canaanite hymn originally sung to Hadad, the god of the storm. In the modified form of the old hymn it is *Yahweh* who manifests his "voice" in the thunderstorm and who is enthroned above the tumult of nature's forces.

The voice of Yahweh is upon the waters;
  the God of glory thunders,
  Yahweh, upon many waters.
The voice of Yahweh is powerful,
  the voice of Yahweh is full of majesty.

  . . . .

The voice of Yahweh flashes forth flames of fire.
The voice of Yahweh shakes the wilderness,
  Yahweh shakes the wilderness of Kadesh.
       —Psalm 29:3-4, 7-8

Another striking example of the borrowing of hymnic elements is the superb creation hymn, Psalm 104. It has long been recognized that this psalm, both in form and content, is related to the beautiful "Hymn to the Aton," which was found in a tomb at Tell el-Amarna, Egypt, the capital of the reforming Pharaoh Akh-en-Aton (Amen-hotep IV: ca. 1380-1362 B.C.). The Egyptian hymn expresses the universal beneficence and recreating power of the sun disc (the Aton). Some scholars maintain that the new style of worship introduced by the iconoclastic Pharaoh was monotheistic. Compare the following excerpt, for instance, with Psalm 104:24:[3]

> *How manifold it is, what thou hast made!*
> *They are hidden from the face (of man).*
> *O sole god, like whom there is no other!*
> *Thou didst create the world according to thy desire,*
> *Whilst thou wert alone:*
> *All men, cattle, and wild beasts,*
> *Whatever is on earth, going upon (its) feet,*
> *And what is on high, flying with its wings.*

During the period of the Davidic monarchy this hymn came to be known in Jerusalem, probably through wisdom circles, and was adapted to the worship of Yahweh, the sole Creator and Lord.

Later on (in chap. 6) we shall have more to say about the way in which the great worship festivals in Jerusalem were influenced by the festivals of Israel's neighbors, such as the New Year festival celebrated in Babylonia. First, however, it is important to focus on what was distinctive in Israel's worship. For, when Israel borrowed literary forms and cultic practices she did not merely imitate her neighbors. Borrowed forms were transformed, religious practices were converted. This is evident from the examples cited above in which hymns from nature religions have been recast to extol Yahweh, whose "glory" is displayed in the realm of nature but who is not the personification of a power of nature.

GOD IN THE HUMAN SITUATION

It would not be surprising if modern men would attempt—like Akhenaton—to turn to the sun disc or some other cosmic phenomenon to express their worship of the Power behind the whole cosmic order. For in modern times the notion has developed—perhaps in a more radical fashion than at any other time in human history —that "God" is outside our historical world. Few people who go to church or synagogue today expect God to manifest his activity in the human situation: the civil rights struggle, the war against poverty and oppression, the tragic suffering of Vietnam, or the harsh political realities of the strife between great world powers. The popular notion is that God is, if not "up there," at least "out there" somewhere—a transcendent being "located in some never-never land beyond the universe." For all practical purposes, such a God is "estranged from the human situation," distant from the places where men are living, suffering, and deciding.[4]

By contrast, Israel's praise did not begin with extolling the Creator whose sovereignty lies before, behind, and above the whole created order. To be sure, the Psalter contains magnificent creation psalms. These include not only Psalm 104, which we have just mentioned, but Psalm 8 with its portrayal of man's elevation to a dignity only a little less than God, and Psalm 19:1-6 with its announcement that day and night the heavens are proclaiming an inaudible anthem to the glory of God. It is not proper to begin our study with these psalms, however, because Israel's worship was not grounded primarily in creation-faith.[5] Rather, Israel began her confession of faith by pointing to a historical situation of distress from which, in a wholly unexpected and humanly impossible way, deliverance was granted. In that situation the reality of God was unveiled.

Unlike other peoples of antiquity, Israel did not find symbols for divine reality in natural or cosmic phenomena: the furious thunderstorm, the mystery of fertility in man, beast, and soil, the splendor of sun, moon, or stars. Rather, Israel turned primarily to *historical symbols*, chief of which was the Exodus from Egypt.

Israel confessed her faith characteristically by recounting the story of her life: "We were once slaves of the mightiest emperor of the day, but Yahweh, the God of our fathers, brought us up out of Egypt and led us into a good and broad land." Thus the people's confession of faith opens, like a symphony pathetique, in a minor mode: the portrayal of a human situation of limitation; and this minor strain is resolved into the major key of praise to the God who opened a way into the future when there was no way.

What we mean by *God*, Israel declares, is this Reality whom we have encountered in our history and who with almighty grace deals with us in the concrete situations of our historical journey. This God, whose name is Yahweh, is not remote and inaccessible; he is the God who makes himself present, who is "with us" (Immanuel). As the prophet Hosea put it, He is "the Holy One in your midst" (Hos. 11:9). And, as the New Testament jubilantly declares, He is the God who is truly and fully present in Jesus Christ, the Lord of the Church. Whether his coming to his people is experienced as judgment or mercy, the saving effect is the same: He opens a way into the future when no way exists. He gives his people a new possibility—in grace. Therefore a cry "out of the depths" resolves into a statement of confidence:

O Israel, hope in Yahweh!
> **For with Yahweh there is steadfast love,**
> **and with him is plenteous redemption.**
> **—Psalm 130:7**

PRAISE IN MINOR AND MAJOR KEYS

In order to understand how minor and major keys are used in the songs of praise to Yahweh, let us turn for a moment to Israel's early creedal statements which blend the motifs of distress and deliverance, humiliation and exaltation. The pattern is clear, for instance, in a passage from the book of Deuteronomy, which many scholars regard as an ancient formulation of Israel's faith.

> *A wandering Aramean was my father; and he went down into Egypt and sojourned there, few in number; and there he became a nation, great, mighty, and populous. And the Egyptians treated us harshly, and afflicted us, and laid upon us hard bondage. Then we cried to Yahweh the God of our fathers, and Yahweh heard our voice, and saw our affliction, our toil, and our oppression; and Yahweh brought us out of Egypt with a mighty hand and an outstretched arm, with great terror, with signs and wonders; and he brought us into this place and gave us this land, a land flowing with milk and honey.*
> —*Deuteronomy 26:5-9*
> (Compare Joshua 24:2-13; Deut. 6:20-23)

This passage is found in a book (Deuteronomy) which received its present form after the fall of Jerusalem in 587 B.C. The language, therefore, is colored by the relatively late "Deuteronomic" style. Yet the *content* of the passage is unquestionably very old, just as the Apostles' Creed, though found in contemporary books of worship and in modern translation, is based on a very early creedal formulation of the Christian church (second century A.D.).

This old credo is not a private prayer. It is, rather, a confession of faith which is made in connection with an act of worship: the presentation of the "first fruits" at the sanctuary (Deut. 26:10). The worshiper who engages in this cultic act of thanksgiving identifies himself with the worshiping community, as indicated by the plural pronouns ("The Egyptians afflicted *us*"; "*We* cried to Yahweh. . . and Yahweh heard *us*," etc.). Even more important for our immediate purpose, the passage expresses the ground of Israel's praise, praise which modulates from the minor into the major key. It begins by portraying a situation of distress. "A wandering Aramean" refers to the patriarch Jacob, and if one paraphrases the original Hebrew more exactly, his wandering is like the "straying" of an animal that has lost its way. The credo continues with a further portrayal of the people's distress in Egypt, out of which "we cried to Yahweh, the God of our fathers." This cry "out of the depths," however, is followed by the jubilant affirmation that "Yahweh heard our voice, and saw our affliction" and marvelously opened a way when there was no way. Thus the appeal out of distress and the jubilant cry of deliverance combine to express Israel's praise of God.

The same motive for the praise of God comes to expression in an old poetic couplet known as the "Song of Miriam." It may have been composed by one who witnessed the event of the crossing of the Sea (not the Red Sea, but a shallow body of water further north in the area of Lake Timsah—in Hebrew called the "Sea of Reeds"). In any case, it is one of the oldest poetic couplets in the Bible.

> "*Sing to Yahweh,*
> *for [ki] he has triumphed gloriously;*
> *the horse and his rider*
> *he has thrown into the sea.*"
> —*Exodus 15:21*

What we have here is the literary genre known as the "hymn"—the oldest example in the Old Testament. The hymn begins with an invitation to the worshiping community (the verb "sing" is in the plural) to join in praise to Yahweh. The motive word (Hebrew: *ki*, translated "for") indicates the ground of Israel's praise. The remainder of the song makes clear the basis of worship. It is not some generalized awareness of God's greatness but rather the display of God's reality in a situation of distress when, humanly speaking, there was no way out. This hymn must have been sung from generation to generation in connection with the recitation of the Exodus story. (See chapt. 5 on the hymn.)

The Exodus story, found in the book of Exodus, chapters 1-15, displays the same structure of oppression and deliverance, humiliation and exaltation. Indeed, the whole story is an enlargement upon the content of Israel's faith as expressed in capsule form in the short credo which we have just considered (Deut. 26:5-9). The Exodus story, too, begins with a cry out of distress as it portrays vividly the oppression of the descendants of Jacob in Egypt (Ex., chapters 1 and 2). The turning point comes in connection with the episode of the "burning bush."

> Then Yahweh said, "I have seen the affliction of my people who are in Egypt, and have heard their cry because of their taskmasters; I know their sufferings, and I have come down to deliver them out of the hand of the Egyptians, and to bring them up out of that land to a good and broad land, a land flowing with milk and honey, . . ."
>
> —*Exodus 3:7-8*

The rest of the story is a narrative portrayal of how Yahweh, the God of the fathers, humbled the mighty and exalted those of low degree (chapters 4-14). The story appropriately concludes with a song of praise (Ex. 15:1-8). This hymn, which in its present form probably comes from the period of the early monarchy, opens by quoting the "Song of Miriam" (Ex. 15:21), though the earlier song is reformulated by transposing the initial verb into the first person: "I will sing." The whole poem is essentially a hymnic elaboration of the ancient song. Thus the Exodus story, from beginning to end, is told to praise and glorify the God who manifested his saving power by creating the historical reality known as Israel and by giving this people a future in his purpose. The story was probably shaped through repetition in the context of liturgical ceremonies, chiefly in the observance of the Passover.

This pattern of humiliation and exaltation can be traced through the whole Bible, especially in liturgical materials. It is found, for instance, in the Song of Deborah (Judges 5), one of the oldest pieces of Hebrew literature of any length, which praises Yahweh for coming to the rescue of his people in a time of desperation when they were threatened by the overwhelming forces of the Canaanites (ca. 1100 B.C.). It is found in the much later "Song of Hannah" (I Sam. 2:1-10), a psalm of thanksgiving for the community's deliverance from deep troubles. And in the New Testament the language of Hannah's song is echoed in the Magnificat (Luke 1:46-55) in which Mary praises the God who exalts the humble and fills the hungry with good things.

> He has shown strength with his arm,
> he has scattered the proud in the imagination of their
> hearts,
> he has put down the mighty from their thrones,
> and exalted those of low degree;
> he has filled the hungry with good things,
> and the rich he has sent empty away.
> He has helped his servant Israel,
> in remembrance of his mercy,

> *as he spoke to our fathers,*
> *to Abraham and to his posterity for ever.*
>
> > —Luke 1:51-55

Indeed, in the New Testament the pattern of humiliation and exaltation finds its deepest expression and widest implication in the gospel of the Crucifixion and Resurrection. The early church proclaimed that in Christ, God has won victory out of defeat and thereby has opened a way for his people into the future, a way in which all men are summoned to walk.

MEDITATIONS UPON GOD'S ACTS IN HISTORY

One of the fundamental differences, then, between Israel's psalms and the songs of her neighbors is that Israel turned primarily to her own historical experience to proclaim the reality of God to the world. The Bible contains the testimony that Israel, God's people, was created *ex nihilo*—out of the "nothingness" of historical oblivion, the chaos of meaningless oppression. Therefore, Yahweh is praised as Israel's *Maker*.

> **O come, let us worship and bow down,**
> > **let us kneel before Yahweh, our Maker!**
> **For he is our God,**
> > **and we are the people of his pasture,**
> > **and the sheep of his hand.**
> > > **—Psalm 95:6-7; cf. 100:3**

So crucial was the Exodus for Israel's existence that it was relived and reactualized from generation to generation. In the great festivals the story of the formation of Israel was told and retold: the deliverance from Egypt, the crossing of the Reed Sea, the wandering in the wilderness, the entrance into Canaan. Eventually the story was supplemented with the narrative of how Yahweh led Israel out of her tribal form of existence into the "modern" form of the state, by raising up David to be king and by making Jerusalem the chosen sanctuary.

It should be emphasized that this whole story was not related as something "back there" in the past. Rather, the story had a meaning for the here and now. It was a drama in which the present generation was involved, existentially. In times of worship the past became present; the worshiper acknowledged that the whole story had happened for him! Accordingly, the faithful Israelite confessed that "Yahweh delivered *us* from Egypt, guided *us* through the great and terrible wilderness, and led *us* into the land of the new beginning." Even today the Passover ritual contains the reminder that every believing Jew should confess that the Lord brought *him* out of Egypt. In the Christian community the believer also confesses that the whole story, which comes to its completion in Jesus Christ, has happened "for me" and "for us." In the sacrament of Holy Communion the event which is crucial for the believing community is contemporized in worship.

This confessional way of retelling the Israelite tradition provides a background for the study of psalms which express the "shared history" of the believing community or—to speak in more theological language—"the history of salvation." The term "salvation history" refers to God's action with his people in the history of Israel—a story which is told confessionally, "for me" and "for us." Since the Christian community has appropriated the story of Israel as its own, it is important to reflect on what is involved in this kind of narrative theology. Some religions, as Amos Wilder reminds us, emphasize philosophical reflection, others mystical meditation, and still others didactic discourse; but "the narrative mode is uniquely important in Christianity."

*It is through the Christian story that God speaks,
and all heaven and earth come into it. God is an active
and purposeful God and his action with and for men
has a beginning, a middle and an end like any good
story. The life of a Christian is not like a dream shot
through with visions and illuminations, but a pilgrimage, a race, in short, a history. The new Christian speech inevitably took the form of a story.*[6]

The "narrative mode" is evident throughout the
Psalter in a number of psalms in which Israel praises
Yahweh by recounting his "deeds of salvation" (e.g.,
Pss. 66:5-7; 71:15-16; 75:1; 77:11-15; 98:1-3; 107:31-
32; 145:4-6). In one group of psalms—sometimes called
"salvation history psalms"—the central subject is the
recitation of Yahweh's "mighty deeds" in Israel's history. One gets the impression from reading and con-
templating these psalms that they have a strong didactic
interest: history is recounted in order to *teach* men the
meaning of their history. These psalms retell the story
of the People of God to show God's *faithfulness*, even
when his people "have erred and strayed from his ways
like lost sheep" and "have followed too much the de-
vices and desires of [their] own hearts"—to quote the
well-known words of the Prayer of General Confession.

It is recommended that these psalms be read in the
following order:[7]

> Psalm 105 A historical summary paralleling the
> Pentateuch from Genesis 12 on
> Psalm 106 A similar summary recited in a peni-
> tential mood
> Psalm 78 A summary which carries the story up
> to the selection of David and the
> choice of Mount Zion (Jerusalem),
> again recited in a penitential style

Psalm 135 A historical summary which includes a reference to Yahweh's power as creator (vss. 5-7)

Psalm 136 An antiphonal summary of Yahweh's great deeds, beginning with the creation

In the present form of the Psalter the first two psalms bracketed together (105 and 106) are regarded as Hallelujah Psalms, that is, each begins and ends with the cultic exclamation, "Praise Yahweh." [8] Here, however, we are not chiefly concerned with how these psalms were classified in the final edition of the Psalter or with their proper classification according to literary type (e.g., "hymn" or "song of thankgiving"). The important thing is their subject matter. These five psalms recapitulate the unfolding drama of Yahweh's dealings with his people from the very beginning of Israel's history to the entrance into the promised land and—in the case of Psalm 78—as far as the raising up of David as the Anointed One. They recite events fundamental to Israel's self-understanding as a people and essential to her knowledge of who God is.

This historical accent in the Psalter holds the possibility of bringing these songs of worship closer to where we live. We, too, are historical beings, and if we are to know God at all, our knowledge will be a historical knowledge. As H. Richard Niebuhr has reminded us: "We are in history as the fish is in water and what we mean by the revelation of God can be indicated only as we point through the medium in which we live." [9] The Christian church has inherited this historical legacy, minus the nationalistic overtones that sounded at times in Israel's Scriptures. In the New Testament, too, the church speaks of God primarily by telling the story of Jesus Christ, a story which is understood to be part of the larger story of God's dealings with his people Israel.

The last pair of psalms bracketed together (135 and 136) have one noteworthy feature in common: they associate the story of Yahweh's deeds on behalf of Israel with his actions as Creator in the beginning. This is true especially of Psalm 136, a historical recitation of Yahweh's mighty deeds, in which the congregation makes an antiphonal response to each affirmation:

For his steadfast love [loyalty]* endures for ever.

(See II Chronicles 7:3, 6 where we find the worshiping congregation responding with this refrain.) Whereas in the first pair the recitation begins with the Exodus (Ps. 106) or with Abraham, Isaac, and Jacob (Ps. 105—the only direct reference to the patriarchs in the Psalter), in Psalm 136 the community traces the actions of God right back to the beginning: to his first work of creating the world (vss. 4-9). This is Israel's way of saying that the meaning disclosed in her own historical experience ("salvation history") unveils the meaning which underlies the whole of human history right from the start, and indeed of the entire cosmos. The "word" which Yahweh spoke to Israel is the same word by which the heavens and the earth were made (Ps. 33:6-9). (See chap. 5.)

CRIES OUT OF A SITUATION OF DISTRESS

In the so-called salvation-history psalms the recapitulation of the story of God's action in the history of his people Israel was not just a paraphrase of the story found in the Pentateuch. Rather, in worship the story was *retold* with a contemporaneous ring, so that it touched the concerns of people in their present situation. It is one thing to affirm that God has done marvelous

---

* "Steadfast love" is the [Revised Standard Version] translation of the Hebrew word ḥesed which means God's "loyalty" to his covenant.

things in the past. For many worshipers, however, the problem is that, if God was marvelously active in the past, why is he apparently inactive in the present, when his people find themselves in deep distress? This is a perennial problem for faith. In the Psalter such distress finds expression in laments in which psalmists, perplexed about the meaning of the present, seek consolation by recalling God's mighty deeds in the past. This is the case in an individual lament:

I will call to mind the deeds of Yahweh,
      yea, I will remember thy wonders of old.
I will meditate on all thy work,
      and muse on thy mighty deeds.
Thy way, O God, is holy.
      What god is great like our God?
Thou art the God who workest wonders,
      who hast manifested thy might among the peoples.
Thou didst with thy arm redeem thy people,
      the sons of Jacob and Joseph.

                    —Psalm 77:11-15

The same note is sounded in community laments, like this one:

We have heard with our ears, O God,
      our fathers have told us,
what deeds thou didst perform in their days,
      in the days of old:
thou with thy own hand didst drive out the nations,
      but them thou didst plant;
thou didst afflict the peoples,
      but them thou didst set free;
for not by their own sword did they win the land,
      nor did their own arm give them victory;
but thy right hand, and thy arm,

**and the light of thy countenance;
for thou didst delight in them.**

—Psalm 44:1-3

Some readers may discount the latter lament on the ground that Israel as a nation had experienced a humiliating defeat at the hand of a political power and was disillusioned because God had not come to their rescue, as he had done when his people were victimized by Pharaoh's tyranny. Such a community lament, it is argued, could be raised by a modern nation which supposes naively that "God is on our side" and which feels "let down" in the political contests of history. Is the problem, however, so simple? Even when we make due allowances for the nationalism in some of the psalms, there is the larger problem that the People of God (*which is not essentially a nation*) lives within the darkness of God's sovereignty in history. Out of this experience arises the poignant question as to why God has apparently forsaken his people. Just because Israel believed so firmly in God's activity in the human situation, she had to learn to praise him in the times of his absence as well as in the times of his presence.

Perhaps we can begin to understand, then, why so many of Israel's psalms are "laments." More than one third of the psalms fall into the category of complaints to God in a situation of limitation and threat (see chap. 3). Indeed, it is striking that all of the psalms which have superscriptions referring to episodes in David's life are laments! Just as Israel in the time of Egyptian oppression cried out for deliverance when the opposing powers were formidable and there was no hope, so in the course of her historical pilgrimage the people again and again cried out to God from the depth of their distress—in the name of David in whom Israel found her existence before God portrayed.

Israel's cries "out of the depths" were not based on the philosophical kind of atheism which men have expressed in the modern period. Now and then psalmists speak about the "fool" who says in his heart, "there is no God" (Ps. 14:1; cf., 10:4). But this is a practical, not a theoretical atheism. The fool does not deny God's reality; he only denies that God's action affects his life. He thinks that God does not see and therefore he can live as he pleases (Ps. 10:11). Helmer Ringgren draws attention in this connection to the old Babylonian phrase "living *ina ramânishu*"—"living by oneself, on one's own resources, without dependence on God." This refusal to "let God be God" is "the essence of sin" and hence the fool and his folly will be exposed in the day when God judges his people.[10]

As can be seen from the salvation history psalms, the God whom Israel worships is praised for his faithfulness and truth. Unlike the capricious gods of the ancient world, the God of Israel is consistent in his purpose and true to his word. Yet in the complexities and ambiguities of historical existence the purpose of God can be seen only dimly. There is no sure evidence which proves that God is in control beyond the shadow of a doubt. Hence the psalmists often cried to God out of their distress, remembering how he had displayed his grace in the past and hoping that he would once again "show his face" graciously. Their lament was a form of praise based on the conviction that God is concerned about his people's condition and that, in ways surpassing human expectation, he answers their cry.

This poor man cried, and Yahweh heard him,
and saved him out of all his troubles.
—Psalm 34:6

Many of the psalms express the stance of "waiting" for God—waiting for the time when he will confirm the reality of his presence and the sovereignty of his purpose in history. The message of Second Isaiah echoes the note struck in many of these psalms:

They who wait for Yahweh shall renew their strength,
  they shall mount up with wings like eagles,
they shall run and not be weary,
  they shall walk and not faint.

—Isaiah 40:31

In our time we can understand this waiting for God, this experience of God's seeming absence from the human situation. It is more difficult for us to understand that Israel's lament out of distress was a way of praising God—in his absence.

In the following discussion we shall not begin with hymns which praise God's greatness in general terms as the Lord of universal history or the Creator of heaven and earth. We shall turn, first, to Israel's speech to God in the form of lament. Since this type of psalm quickly resolves into the assurance that Yahweh hears men's cry, we shall turn next to the songs of thanksgiving. Then in later chapters we shall study the hymns which extol the greatness and glory of God, who is enthroned as King over Israel, the nations, and the entire creation.

3:

MURMURINGS
IN THE ABSENCE
OF GOD

Israel's worship was evoked by the action of the God who turned to his people in their oppression and in a marvelous way opened to them a new possibility of life. Accordingly, the faith of the psalmists does not rest upon glittering generalities about the nature of God or upon a numinous awareness of his majesty in the remote reaches of the universe; rather, it is founded upon the good news that God makes himself present in the midst of history to help his people.

Yahweh works vindication
    and justice for all who are oppressed.
He made known his ways to Moses,
    his acts to the people of Israel.
               —Psalm 103:6-7

Therefore the community is addressed with an imperative: "Sing to Yahweh!" [1]

The story of Yahweh's turning toward his people, as found in the Exodus tradition (Exodus 1-15), is supplemented with the narrative of Israel's murmurings in the wilderness. According to traditions found in the books of Exodus (16, 17, and 32), Numbers (11, 14, 16, 20, 21), and Deuteronomy (e.g., 8), the wilderness sojourn was the time when Israel's faith was under trial. To be sure, "signs" of Yahweh's presence were given, such as the manna which fell from the desert bushes, the quails that drifted into the area with the prevailing winds, or the water that was found in unexpected places. These signs, however, were indications but not proofs of God's presence and guidance. Indeed, the period in the wilderness was a time when the people longed for the "fleshpots" of Egypt and when they murmured, "Is Yahweh among us, or not?" (Ex. 17:7)

This portrayal of Israel in the wilderness was not so much a recital of ancient history as a mirror in which the people found its own history with God reflected. In the same mirror the pilgrim People of God of the New Testament period saw itself. Paul, for instance, did not dismiss the events of the wilderness as ancient history but insisted that "these things were written down for our instruction upon whom the end of the ages has come" (I Cor. 10:11). The signs given to God's people by Christ were not proofs of God's real presence and his sovereign control of history beyond any shadow of a doubt; they were assurances given to faith. God's sovereignty in Christ has a darkness which baffles human comprehension; and within this "valley of deep shadow" (Ps. 23:4) God's people walk.

THE LITERATURE OF LAMENTATION

It is not surprising, then, that the Bible contains a great deal of literature of lamentation. Embedded in the book of Jeremiah are six "confessions" or laments in which the prophet complains to God in strong language, protests his innocence, and cries out for vindication over his enemies: i) 11:18-12:6; ii) 15:10-21; iii) 17:14-18; iv) 18:19-23; v) 20:7-13; vi) 20:14-18. A good example is the second lament (ii). Like Hamlet, Jeremiah castigates his mother for having borne him (cf. Job 3); he cries out for vengeance upon his persecutors; he accuses God of having become like a "deceitful brook" which is full during the spring rains but dries up in the summer; and at the end he is given an oracle in which Yahweh assures him of deliverance.

The fact that Jeremiah raised such cries of dereliction gave rise to the later tradition that he was the author of the mournful poems in the Book of Lamentations, composed in the shadow of the destruction of Jerusalem by the Babylonians in 587 B.C. Three of these poems (Lam. 1, 2, 4) are really funeral dirges which open with the customary wail 'ekah (translated "how," e.g., Lam. 1:1) and are cast in the "limping 3/2 meter" used in songs of mourning. The other two poems, however, are laments in form: chapter 3 an individual lament and chapter 5 a community lament.

In this connection mention should also be made of the Book of Job, a wisdom writing. Although the prose introduction and conclusion to this book portray a pious man who took all manner of hardships meekly and patiently, the poetic sections depict a figure who, in language even stronger than that of Jeremiah, lashes out against God, protests his innocence, and cries out for vindication.

As has been noted, laments far outnumber any other kind of songs in the Psalter. It is striking that the laments found in Jeremiah's confessions, the Book of Job, and the Book of Lamentations have the same general form as the laments found in the Psalter. This suggests that all these writers were following an accepted literary convention, as poets frequently do in our Western culture. The form was not confined to Israelite society but was known throughout the ancient Near East. Israel's psalms of lament display a formal resemblance to the songs of her neighbors, especially the Babylonians and Assyrians. This may be seen, for instance, from the magnificent "Prayer of Lamentation to Ishtar" [2] which comes from the neo-Babylonian period (approximately the time of Jeremiah). It begins with a long ascription of praise to Ishtar, the Queen of Heaven "who guides mankind aright" and who "regards the oppressed and mistreated." The second movement of the prayer is a lament in affliction to "the goddess of goddesses":

> Let the favor of thine eyes be upon me.
> With thy bright features look faithfully upon me.
> Drive away the evil spells of my body (and) let me see thy bright light.
> How long, O my Lady, shall my adversaries be looking upon me,
> In lying and untruth shall they plan evil against me,
> Shall my pursuers and those who exult over me rage against me?
> How long, O my Lady, shall the crippled and weak seek me out?
> One has made for me long sackcloth; thus I have appeared before thee.
> The weak have become strong; but I am weak.
> I toss about like flood-water, which an evil wind makes violent.
> My heart is flying; it keeps fluttering like a bird of heaven.
> I mourn like a dove night and day.
> I am beaten down, and so I weep bitterly.
> With "Oh" and "Alas" my spirit is distressed.
> I—what have I done, O my god and my goddess?
> Like one who does not fear my god and my goddess I am treated;
> While sickness, headache, loss, and destruction are provided for me;
> So are fixed upon me terror, disdain, and fullness of wrath,

Anger, choler, and indignation of gods and men.

The suppliant, after pleading that he has been devoted faithfully to Ishtar, cries out for deliverance.

> *Accept the abasement of my countenance; hear my prayers.*
> *Faithfully look upon me and accept my supplication.*
> *How long, O my Lady, wilt thou be angered so that thy face is turned away?*
> *How long, O my Lady, wilt thou be infuriated so that thy spirit is enraged?*
> *Turn thy neck which thou hast set against me; set thy face [toward] good favor.*
> *Like the water of the opening up of a canal let thy emotions be released.*
> *My foes like the ground let me trample;*
> *Subdue my haters and cause them to crouch down under me.*
> *Let my prayers and my supplications come to thee.*
> *Let thy great mercy be upon me.*
> *Let those who see me in the street magnify thy name.*

The general structure of this Babylonian psalm (address of praise, complaint, protest of innocence, petition for deliverance, and concluding vow of praise) corresponds closely to Israelite psalms of lament. In fact, we must assume that this cultic form, mediated through the Canaanites, influenced Israelite worship very early, probably during the two centuries before David (1200-1000 B.C.) when Israel was occupying the land. There are, however, profound differences in content. The observation that the Ishtar psalm is polytheistic, while Israelite psalms are addressed to the one God, is true enough, but does not go to the root of the matter. The Babylonian psalm was to be accompanied by a ritual of incantation, that is, a magical spell over the evil spirits (demons). Thus prayer was tied up with magic—the release of a power believed to be effective in overcoming evil. The worshiper found himself in a situation of caprice, in which he was not sure what he had done wrong and not certain whether the goddess could deliver him from evil. He was apprehensive in the face of the hostile powers that make life precarious. By contrast, the Israelite psalms of lament express the conviction that Yahweh is trustworthy and faithful. He has shown his mercy decisively in rescuing his people from Egyptian oppression and by displaying his saving purpose in the subsequent crises of their history. He is true to his word, and his word has the power to accomplish his purpose. Therefore, it is unnnecessary to use magic to assist him or cajole him to rescue his people from distress.

Nevertheless, the People of God always finds itself in the interim between God's promise and the fulfillment of the promise. That interim is the time when faith is put to the test; for there are no unambiguous proofs that God has spoken and that he is in control of the human situation. This is the problem with which God's people wrestle throughout the Old Testament period—and beyond. The hymns found among the writings of the Qumran monastery (the Dead Sea scriptures), which flourished at the beginning of the Christian era, contain the same notes of lament, the same motif of "the wilderness of isolation." [3] The New Testament, of course, proclaims that God has spoken decisively in Jesus Christ, thereby ratifying and fulfilling the promises made to Israel. But the Christian community also finds itself living in the interim between the inauguration of God's Kingdom and its final realization, between the first break of dawn and the full light of day. Therefore it knows the trial of faith which is poignantly expressed in the laments of the Psalter. It is reported that Jesus himself uttered the words of one of the laments as a cry of dereliction from the cross: "My God, why hast thou forsaken me?" (Ps. 22:1; see Matt. 27:46 and Mark 15:34); and he died with the words of another lament on his lips: "Into thy hand I commit my spirit" (Ps. 31:5; see Luke 23:46). Thus, Israel's lamentations were drawn into the context of the Passion Story and thereby into the history of the People of God which received a new beginning in Jesus Christ.

THE SITUATION OF THE LAMENT

The first thing to notice about the laments in the Psalter is that they fall into two general groups: laments of the community and laments of the individual. The boundary between the two is uncertain for sometimes, as in Psalm 129, Israel speaks in the first personal pronoun; and at other times, as in Psalm 77, the individual identifies himself with the affliction of Israel and laments for the community. Nevertheless, the following outlines of these two groups of Psalms are useful here. Those marked with an asterisk deserve special attention.

COMMUNITY LAMENTS

*12 "The faithful have vanished from among the sons of men"
*44 "For thy sake we are slain all the day long"
 58 "Surely there is a God who judges on earth"
 60 "Thou hast made thy people suffer hard things"
 74 "O God, why dost thou cast us off forever?"
 79 "The heathen have come into thy inheritance"
*80 "Restore us, O Lord God of hosts!"
 83 "O God, do not keep silence"
*85 "Righteousness and peace will kiss each other"
*90 "Yahweh, thou hast been our dwelling place in all generations"

*94 "Thou God of vengeance, shine forth!"
123 "Our eyes look to Yahweh our God"
126 "May those who sow in tears reap with shouts
of joy!" (possibly not a lament)
129 "Sorely have they afflicted me from my youth"
137 "By the waters of Babylon, there we sat down
and wept"
(See also the community lament in Lamentations 5.)

All of these psalms express the distress of the community in a time of threat when it seemed that the odds
were against believing that God was with his people.
One psalm, Psalm 137, clearly reflects the period of
the Babylonian Exile (587-538 B.C.). For the most part,
however, the community laments are couched in general
terms which allowed them to be used in recurring cultic situations, especially in the cultic "fast" held at times
of political crisis (Judges 20:26; I Sam. 7:6; I Kings
21:9-12).

A passage in II Chronicles 20:3-4 gives a vivid picture of the "situation in life" of the community lament.
The country was under threat of military invasion.

*Then Jehoshaphat feared, and set himself to seek
Yahweh, and proclaimed a fast throughout all Judah.
And Judah assembled to seek help from Yahweh; from
all the cities of Judah they came to seek Yahweh.*

The story goes that while the congregation was engaged
in a "lament," crying to Yahweh in their affliction and
entreating him to execute judgment upon the invaders
(vss. 5-12), a prophet stood up to speak "words of assurance":

*Thus says Yahweh to you: "Fear not, and be not dis-
mayed at this great multitude; for the battle is not*

yours but God's. . . . Fear not, and be not dismayed;
tomorrow go out against them, and Yahweh will be
with you."

Then Jehoshaphat bowed his head with his face to
the ground, and all Judah and the inhabitants of Je-
rusalem fell down before Yahweh, worshiping Yah-
weh. And the Levites, of the Kohathites and the
Korahites, stood up to praise Yahweh, the God of
Israel, with a very loud voice.
—II Chronicles 20:3-4, 15, 17-19

The prophecy of Joel, delivered at a time when a locust plague threatened the land, presupposes this cultic tradition. The prophet summoned the people to repentance:

Sanctify a fast,
> *call a solemn assembly.*
Gather the elders
> *and all the inhabitants of the land*
to the house of Yahweh your God;
> *and cry to Yahweh!*
—Joel 1:14; cf. 2:12-17

In this context is preserved the actual lament which the priests were to utter on the occasion, a lament which strikes the note heard in community laments in the Psalter:

Between the vestibule and the altar
> *let the priests, the ministers of Yahweh, weep*
and say, "Spare thy people, O Yahweh,
> *and make not thy heritage a reproach,*
> *a byword among the nations.*
Why should they say among the peoples,
> *'Where is their God?'"*
—Joel 2:17

More numerous are the individual laments. Original-ly these laments were composed by individuals who, in a time of need or anxiety, went to the temple to pray to Yahweh. Consider, for instance, the case of Hannah. Having had no child, she went to the temple (once located at Shiloh) and in "great anxiety and vexation" poured out her heart to Yahweh. In this cultic situation the priest, Eli, spoke "words of assurance" to her: "Go in peace, and the God of Israel grant your petition which you have made to him" (I Sam. 1:3-20). We may assume that many of the psalms of individual lament presuppose a setting in worship something like this, though in the course of time they lost their cultic association and be-came only forms of literary composition. The super-scription to Psalm 102, one of the "penitential psalms," is an appropriate introduction to all these laments: "A prayer of one afflicted, when he is faint and pours out his complaint before Yahweh."

INDIVIDUAL LAMENTS

*3	"Many are saying of me, there is no help for him in God"
*4	"In peace I will both lie down and sleep" (song of trust?)
5	"Lead me, O Yahweh, in thy righteousness"
7	"Establish thou the righteous"
9-10	"Yahweh is a stronghold for the oppressed"
13	"How long, O Yahweh? Wilt thou forget me for ever?"
14 and 53	"The fool says in his heart, 'There is no God'"
17	"From thee let my vindication come!"
*22	"My God, why hast thou forsaken me?"
25	"Make me to know thy ways, O Yahweh"
26	"Thy steadfast love is before my eyes"
27:7-14	"Forsake me not, O God of my salvation!"

(The first part of the psalm is a song of trust)

28 "If thou be silent to me"

*31 "Into thy hand I commit my spirit"

35 "Contend, O Yahweh, with those who contend with me"

*39 "I am thy passing guest"

40:12-17 "Be pleased, O Yahweh, to deliver me" (cf. Ps. 70) (The first part of the psalm is an individual thanksgiving.)

41 "Heal me, for I have sinned against thee!"

*42-43 "Why are you cast down, O my soul?"

52 "Why do you boast, O mighty man?"

53 See Psalm 14

54 "Save me, O God, by thy name"

55 "Cast your burden on Yahweh and he will sustain you"

56 "My enemies trample upon me all day long"

*57 "I cry . . . to God who fulfills his purpose for me"

59 "Deliver me from my enemies, O my God"

61 "Lead thou me to the rock that is higher than I"

64 "Preserve my life from dread of the enemy"

69 "I have come into deep waters"

70 and 40:13-17 "May all who seek thee rejoice and be glad"

*71 "Upon thee I have leaned from my birth"

*77 "I will call to mind the deeds of Yahweh"

86 "Teach me thy way, O Yahweh"

88 "Dost thou work wonders for the dead?"

89 "Where is thy steadfast love . . .?" (royal lament)

109 "In return for my love they accuse me"

120 "Too long have I had my dwelling among those who hate peace"

*139 "Whither shall I flee from thy presence?"

140 "I know that Yahweh mantains the cause of the afflicted"

141 "In thee I seek refuge; leave me not defenseless!"
142 "No refuge remains to me, no man cares for me"
(See also the individual lament in Lamentations 3.)

In a number of psalms of lament the affliction is a deep sense of sin, out of which the suppliant pleads for God's healing grace. In the liturgical tradition of the church these psalms have been bracketed together as "penitential psalms" (Pss. 6 [32], 38, 51, 102, 130, 143).

THE FORM OF THE LAMENT

The term "lament" is not an altogether satisfactory label for these psalms. The word may suggest a pessimistic view of life, a morbid concentration on human agony or guilt. But this is not the mood of the psalmists. "All the Psalmists," as Christoph Barth observes, "are concerned not with distress as such, but with taking it before God, who they know is the judge and at the same time the redeemer, with sovereign power over all distress." [4] These psalmists cry to God out of the depths in the confidence and certainty that he has the power to lift a person out of the "miry bog" and set his feet upon a rock (Ps. 40:1-2). Hence the laments are really expressions of praise—praise offered to God in the time of his absence.

Here we can do little more than delineate the form of the lament, in the hope that this will provide a basis for the reader to study the psalms on his own—especially those psalms marked with an asterisk in the lists above. In the case of the lament, as we have observed, Israel borrowed a cultic form known in the ancient world and poured into it the content of her faith in Yahweh. While subject to variation according to the interests and creativity of the author, the form exhibits a definite structure. See if you can trace the elements of the form in a selected lament, such as Psalm 22.

A. Address to God
Sometimes a brief cry, though this may be expanded into an ascription of praise (Ps. 9:1-2) or the recollection of God's deeds of old (Ps. 44:1-8).

B. Complaint
(1) In community laments the distress may be military crisis, drought, famine, scourge (cf. I Kings 8:33-40); in individual laments the problem may be sickness, threat of enemies, fear of death, etc. In penitential psalms, the distress is awareness of sin (Ps. 38:4, 18).
(2) Often the complaint is accompanied by a protestation of innocence (Ps. 17:3-5) or a plea for forgiveness.

C. Confession of Trust
An expression of confidence in God in spite of the problematic situation; often introduced by an adversative "but," "nevertheless" (e.g., Ps. 3:3-6).

D. Petition
The psalmist appeals to God to intervene and deliver, sometimes adducing grounds to support his appeal (e.g., Ps. 6:4-5).

E. Words of Assurance
The psalmist's expression of trust finds expression in the certainty that his prayer will be heard. In some laments we deduce that "words of assurance" were actually spoken by a priest or prophet (e.g., Ps. 12:5), thus preparing the way for the concluding vow of praise.

F. Vow of Praise
In the confidence that God hears and answers, the suppliant vows to call upon the name of Yahweh and to testify before the community what He has

done (Pss. 7:17; 13:6). In cases where the lament includes "words of assurance," the psalm ends with exclamations of praise (Ps. 6:8-10).

As can be seen from this outline, these cries out of distress are motivated by the deep confidence that God is an active God who intervenes to deliver. Therefore, the movement of the lament is toward the song of thanksgiving (to be considered in the next chapter). Some of the psalms in the Psalter are essentially elaborations of a motif found in the lament. For instance, the protestation of innocence is prominent in some psalms (Pss. 7, 17, 26), and the cry for vindication in others (Pss. 69, 109). In still others, as we shall see presently, the laments are deepened into penitential prayers. And the songs of trust (see chap. 7) are essentially expansions of the confession of trust which is an essential part of the lament.

Since the lament covers essential aspects of Israel's service of worship, it would be instructive to compare this cultic form with the elements of Christian orders of worship.

Address   (Invocation, Call to Worship)
Complaint   (Prayer of General Confession)
Confession of Trust   (The Creed)
Petition for Deliverance   (Congregational Prayers,
                                            The Lord's Prayer)
Oracle of Assurance   (The Sermon)
Vow of Praise   (Concluding Hymn or Doxology)

THE PROBLEM OF THE "ENEMIES" IN THE PSALMS

One of the thorniest problems in the psalms of lament is the fact that "enemies" have a central place in prayer to God. Who are these enemies? In the case of the community laments the question is not difficult to answer.

Laments of this type were used on fast days when the community was threatened by military foes, famine or drought, or some pestilence such as a locust plague (cf. the Book of Joel). Solomon's temple prayer (I Kings 8:33-40) gives a clear picture of the kinds of threat to the people which occasioned community laments.

In the case of the individual laments, however, we can never be sure what is troubling the psalmist, for he resorts to picturesque language to describe his concrete condition. Psalm 22 is a good example. The psalmist finds himself encompassed by "strong bulls of Bashan" (vs. 12); he is "poured out like water" and his heart melts like wax (vs. 14); and he is laid "in the dust of death" (vs. 15). In shifting imagery he declares that he is attacked by dogs, lions, wild oxen, the sword (vss. 16-21). It is hard to tell from this language whether the suppliant is suffering from sickness, anxiety over death, personal attack by ungodly people, or some other disgrace.

Various attempts have been made to identify these enemies. It has been suggested, for instance, that the laments presuppose a situation of party strife within the Israelite community, like that which broke out in the Maccabean period between the orthodox Jews and those who favored the Greeks. Another proposal is that some of these psalms are "prayers of the accused" (Pss. 7, 35, 57, 69) made during a legal investigation in the sanctuary. In the presence of the highest Judge the accused raised his cry for help, protested his innocence, threw himself confidently on the mercy of the divine court and, when a favorable divine verdict was given, raised his voice in thanksgiving. Another suggestion is that the "evil doers" were magicians who, by working a magic spell, brought sickness or calamity upon hapless victims.

> His mouth is filled with cursing and deceit and oppression,
> > under his tongue are mischief and iniquity.
> He sits in ambush in the villages;
> > in hiding places he murders the innocent.
> > > —Psalm 10:7-8

None of these interpretations is completely satisfactory. The plain truth is that we really do not know who the enemies were, for the psalmist expresses his distress in stylized language which had been employed for centuries in cultic situations. Indeed, it is striking that the Babylonian psalms of lament used the same conventional imagery (engulfing billows of the flood, miring into the waters of a swamp, descent into the pit, attack by wild beasts, etc.) and even left a blank to be filled in with the name of the worshiper who chose to use the psalm![5] This explains why the enemies in the individual laments are so faceless, and it also helps to account for the fact that these psalms are usable by many different people in times of trouble. The psalmist does not talk boringly about the details of his personal situation (like the proverbial person who inflicts the story of his operation on his friends); he does not turn introspectively to his own inner life. Rather, by using conventional language he affirms that his situation is *typical* of every man who struggles with the meaning of his life in the concrete situations of tension, hostility, and conflict. That is why these psalms have been used down through the centuries by suppliants who cry to God out of their concrete situation. They seem to leave a blank, as it were, for the insertion of your own personal name.

THE CRY FOR VINDICATION

More problematical is the fact that these psalmists— like the prophet Jeremiah in his laments (see especially Jer. 20:7-12)—cry out to God for vindication and even pray for vengeance against the enemies, whoever they are. A number of these psalms are often called "imprecatory" or "cursing" psalms (Pss. 35, 59, 69, 70, 109, 137, 140; and in the category of community laments Pss. 12, 58, 83 strike the same note). Two of these psalms—Psalm 69 and, especially, Psalm 109—are very difficult to use in Christian worship. It is often said that the language of these psalms is sub-Christian, having no place in the "new age" governed by the commandment of the Sermon on the Mount, "Love your enemies and pray for those who persecute you" (Matt. 5:44). For many people the magnificent 139th Psalm is ruined by the thought expressed in verses 19-22 ("Do I not hate them that hate thee, O Yahweh? . . . I hate them with perfect hatred."). The most conspicuous example of imprecation is the closing passage of Psalm 137, a folk song which cried out for vengeance against the Babylonians who destroyed the nation Judah in 587 B.C. and the Edomites who assisted them in the sack of Jerusalem (cf. Obadiah 10-14).

Remember, O Yahweh against the Edomites
    the day of Jerusalem,
how they said, "Rase it, rase it!
    Down to its foundations!"
O daughter of Babylon, you devastator!
    Happy shall he be who requites you
    with what you have done to us!
Happy shall he be who takes your little ones
    and dashes them against the rock!
        —Psalm 137:7-9

It is surely a debatable question as to whether the church should retain the whole Psalter in its worship, including these troublesome passages, or whether the Psalter should be censored at those points which seem to be inconsistent with God's revelation in Jesus Christ. It would be interesting to check the responsive readings included in modern hymnals or books of worship, to see the degree to which the Psalms have been edited for Christian worship. Before this question is answered too quickly, however, the voice of contemporary theologians should be heard. Dietrich Bonhoeffer advocated the daily use, especially in our morning and evening devotions, of *all* the psalms. It was his view that we should not "pick and choose" for "otherwise we dishonor God by presuming to know better than he what we should pray." Similarly Christoph Barth objects to the "impropriety" of omitting certain passages which offend us (e.g., Ps. 104:35 or Ps. 139:19-22) and insists: "It is impossible to have the Psalter without its reference to the godless enemies." [6]

Now, it can readily be admitted that the laments of the Psalter are raised from the depths of human anxiety, from which the emotions of bitterness and hatred often well up. The Psalter, like the Old Testament as a whole, is "of the earth, earthy." All the moods and passions of human life find expression here. The Psalms do not point to a trans-historical world of pure ideals—the good, the true, and the beautiful; rather, they are concerned with the historical scene of change, struggle, and suffering where God meets men and lays his claim upon them. Psalm 137, quoted above, comes out of a situation of historical struggle where a small people found itself overwhelmed by the massed might of an empire and was suddenly deprived of everything held precious. The church cannot automatically join in this psalm. Yet we must remind ourselves that Psalm 137 has found many parallels in modern life, for instance, during World War II when the pride of France was violated by Hitler's armies, or when brave little Finland was overrun by Russian forces. The question is whether these all too human cries have a place in man's speech to God.

We have noticed that the laments use a stylized language which was capable of being reinterpreted in the ever-new situations in which the worshiping community found itself. In describing the enemies in this traditional language, with its monotonous and exaggerated epithets, the psalmists were not calling for a personal fight; rather, they were concerned about the adversaries of the cause of God. Indeed, there is a strong tendency to associate the enemies with the powers of chaos who have opposed God's purpose from the time of creation and on. This helps us to understand why the psalmists think of the enemies ("the wicked," "the godless," "the workers of evil") as *God's enemies* who, as such, are to be hated. "The imagery being mythological," writes Helmer Ringgren, "the enemies are taken to be more than human; they become the representatives of all evil forces that threaten life and order in the world"—the order which the Creator continues to uphold against all the threatening powers of chaos.[7]

The Gospels of the New Testament portray man's distress as arising from the threat of demonic powers, organized—according to the language of the myth—into an oppressive empire under the rule of Satan. According to this imaginative way of thinking, man's problem is not just the frustration that arises out of his own personal life; rather, he experiences the threat of evil powers which are external to him, which affect him in the society in which he lives, and which may seduce him in a time of testing (temptation). In the Lord's Prayer we are taught to pray: "Lead us not into temptation, but deliver us from evil (the Evil One)." We can understand the intention of this language in our time when people, perhaps more than any other period of human history, find themselves to be victims of structures of power, of antagonisms or prejudices embodied in social customs and behavior, of tremendous social forces or "isms" before which the individual feels helpless. Thus, in the last century, the laments of Negro spirituals expressed "one continual cry" [8] against oppressive pharaohs, and more recently a similar sense of frustration has found expression in the folk songs of young "prophets with guitars." The psalmists' cry for vindication may be closer to our lives than we realize. Man cries out for justice in the social structures of human society—a justice which would somehow give corporate expression to love.

THE VENGEANCE THAT IS GOD'S

In trying to answer the questions raised by "the psalms of vengeance" several things must be kept in mind. First, it is important to consider how biblical language is used, that is, the syntax within which words like "avenge, vengeance" function. It is too bad that these words are translated from the Hebrew by English words which in our thought-world have a negative connotation. No one wants to be regarded as "vengeful" and therefore it hardly seems right to apply the term to God! However, the Hebrew verb *naqam* [vindicate] has the basic meaning of "save" in the Old Testament, as it had in other ancient literature, and therefore can be used in exactly the same sense as the Hebrew verb *yasha'* from which the noun "salvation" comes. The language presupposes the view that God has entered into covenant relation with his people and within the terms of that relationship he acts as Judge or Vindicator to defend and uphold justice. Therefore his subjects, within the terms of the covenant, appeal to the Suzerain for help, vindication, "salvation." When considered in this light, it is understandable that *"naqam* [to vindicate] is the sole prerogative of God." [9] And this is precisely what we read in the New Testament:

> *Beloved, never avenge yourselves, but leave it to the wrath of God; for it is written, "Vengeance is mine, I will repay, says the Lord."*
>
> —*Romans 12:19 (echoing Deut. 32:35)*
> *See also Hebrews 10:30*

In view of this, it is doubtful whether these psalms should be described as "imprecatory" or cursing psalms. In the ancient world, as in some undeveloped societies today, it was believed that the word spoken in curse released a power, or spell, which was automatically effective. (Remember the story in Numbers 22-24 about the diviner Balaam whom Balak, the king of Moab, employed to destroy Israel with the power of the curse.) As long as one believed in the power of "verbal vengeance," prayer was unnecessary.

> *The distinctiveness of the curse lies in the fact that it is aimed* directly, *without any detour via God, at the one it is meant to hit. A curse is a word of power which the swearer released without recourse to God.*[10]

The Psalter, it is true, contains traces of ancient curse formulas (e.g., Ps. 58:6-9) which probably were dependent upon traditional language used in cultic ceremonies of covenant renewal; but no longer are they curses in the proper sense. They are really prayers to God who obtains vindication in his own way and in his own time.

Another thing to consider is that the Old Testament Psalms wrestle with the problems of human existence within the context of this life—the "three score years and ten" of Psalm 90:10. Lacking the eschatological horizon of the New Testament, they concentrate on the problems of life *now* with a fierce and passionate intensity. The psalmists do not take seriously the possibility that the imbalances of life will somehow be corrected in another form of existence beyond our historical experience. God's dealings with men are confined to this earthly life. For them, as for many modern people, death is the final limitation; accordingly, the answers to the question of existence must be found now. They thirst for God in the present, and seek the satisfaction of that thirst in the historical arena. In the New Testament, of course, this barrier is broken through. There the good news rings out that in Jesus Christ, God has conquered the power of death and has thrown open the door into the future. But this victory is only a foretaste of the final consummation when God's action as Judge (Vindicator) will take place. Thus the parable about the unrighteous judge, to whom a widow came persistently with the plea "Vindicate me against my adversary," ends with the interpretation:

And will not God vindicate his elect, who cry to him day and night? Will he delay long over them? I tell you, he will vindicate them speedily. Nevertheless, when the Son of man comes, will he find faith on earth?

—Luke 18:7-8

The Christian church reads the psalmists' cries for vindication in the larger context of the whole Bible which reaches a climax with the announcement that the Vindicator has already responded to his people's cries in Jesus Christ. The New Testament witnesses that Christ has experienced man's cry "out of the depths." Not only does Christ pray with us in all human suffering but he enables men to have a confidence which makes them "more than conquerors" (Rom. 8:31-39).

In the church's liturgical tradition, which goes back into the Middle Ages, seven psalms have been singled out as penitential psalms, because they express man's humility before God. All of them should be read carefully.

PENITENTIAL PSALMS

    *6   "Deliver me, for the sake of thy steadfast love"

[*32] "Blessed is he whose transgression is forgiven†" (song of thanksgiving)

  *38 "There is no health in my bones because of my sin"

  *51 "Create in me a clean heart, O God"

*102 "My days are like an evening shadow"

*130 "Out of the depths I cry to thee, O Yahweh!"

*143 "No man living is righteous before thee"

At first glance, these psalms seem to clash with other psalms which express the innocence of the suppliant, for instance:

Yahweh judges the peoples;
> **judge [vindicate] me, O Yahweh, according to my righteousness**
and according to the integrity that is in me.
>> **—Psalm 7:8 (cf. 26:1)**

Pleas of this kind are usually accompanied by the protestations of innocence which are noticeable in some psalms (Pss. 17:3-5; 18:20-24; 26:1-7; 41:12; 59:3-4). These psalmists declare that if Yahweh searches or tests the heart, he will find no "wickedness." This seems to be the assumption of the 139th Psalm whose conclud-

† The favorite psalm of Augustine.

ing verses are often quoted with great approval (vss. 23-24). These psalms which plead man's righteousness seem to be irreconcilable with those that begin with a penitent cry:

Have mercy on me, O God,
> according to thy steadfast love;
according to thy abundant mercy
> blot out my transgressions.
> > —Psalm 51:1

The question ought to be explored as to whether the psalms of "innocence" are in absolute conflict with the psalms of "penitence." As Bonhoeffer remarked, "The notion that we can never suffer innocently so long as within us there still hides some kind of defect is a thoroughly unbiblical and demoralizing thought." [11] In facing this question we should therefore divest ourselves of notions of righteousness which we have inherited from our culture, largely under Greek and Roman influence. Normally we assume that a "righteous" person is one who conforms to some legal or moral standard; such a person is held to be righteous according to the law ("law" here being interpreted in terms of Greek *nomos* or Roman *lex*).

Another view of righteousness is illustrated in the story found in Genesis 15:1-6. Abraham could not see how he (and the People of God) could have a future when he had no son, and the only legal heir was his household servant. How could God possibly be true to his promise when, humanly speaking, there was no possibility of fulfillment? The story goes that Abraham was led outside his tent, where he could view the myriads of stars. With no other evidence than the stars in the sky, Abraham was assured that his descendants would be myriad. Then comes a crucial sentence: "He believed [better: "put his trust in"] Yahweh; and he [Yahweh] reckoned ["imputed," "imparted," "accorded"] it to him as righteousness" (Gen. 15:6).

This story makes it clear that "righteousness"—in the sense that Israel uses the term—is being *in right relation* with God, that is, trusting in his word. Such a relationship is not an achievement of man; it is something that God initiates. Therefore, the passage in Genesis 15 asserts that this "right relation" was imputed, accorded, or granted as a gift by God. More and more we are coming to realize that such a passage presupposes a cultic situation—as reflected in the psalms of righteousness (innocence)—in which God accepts a man as "righteous," that is, as being in a trustful relationship, and therefore imparts to him "righteousness," that is, the status of a right relationship. This idea of righteousness (right-relationship), as something which man does not assert but which is *given* (cf. Ps. 85:10-11), dominates the New Testament. Paul insists that righteousness is not something a man achieves but is a free gift, something that is accorded to him in Christ. Therefore he wants to stand before God "not having a righteousness of my own, based on law, but that which is through faith in Christ, the righteousness from God that depends on faith" (Phil. 3:9). Thus the Christian church experiences in its own way what members of the Israelite community experienced in worship: the divine recognition of "righteousness," or the right relationship of trust and dependence upon God which amounts to "salvation." The alternative attitude toward God was expressed by the "wicked," "the fools" who supposed that they could live out of their own resources, as though God were not to be reckoned with.

Righteousness, then, does not mean being without defect in the presence of God. If that were the case, the so-called psalms of penitence could not be prayed by the worshiping community. The strange thing is that it is the "righteous," "the pious," "the faithful," "the innocent" who pray the so-called penitential psalms. For it is only when one stands in a right relationship with God—that is, having a righteousness which he cannot claim as his prerogative but which is granted to him in the relationship of the Covenant—that he can assert his innocence before men and plead for God's forgiveness. "It is the righteous who confess their unrighteousness before God," writes Christoph Barth, "only the godless man refuses to do this, because he regards himself as righteous." We are left, then, with the apparent paradox of "the righteousness of the sinner." [12]

THE HIDDENNESS OF GOD

The psalms of lament lead us finally to the deepest dimension of the witness of the Bible: faith's acknowledgment that the God who reveals himself in history remains hidden. He does not become the prisoner of men's thoughts or the captive of their schemes, nor is his purpose easily discernible in the unfolding drama of human history. Living in the space between promise and fulfillment, men of faith are torn between the No and the Yes. In the New Testament we find that the very place where God's victory is manifest—the Cross—is the place where the shadows are deepest. Jesus appropriately takes the laments of the Psalter into his own suffering with us. To be sure, the darkness is illumined by the dawn of Easter morning; but the darkness remains as a trial for faith.

It is understandable that in our time, when faith is subjected to the trial of living in the time of "the eclipse of God" (Martin Buber), men have learned to compose their own psalms of lament. Here, for instance, is a contemporary lament composed by one of the author's students:[13]

O Lord, were there a language in our language
        with which I might praise Your nameless
        name.
The language of Your creation has lost its power
        on our controlling words of technic progress.
Your word of might we match against our dominion
        with real chance we may be victors.
Your sword is no power to our warring,
        Your hand was blown atomically from the
        earth.
Only Your hollowed name remained
        to bless our every action
For "if God is for us, who can be against us?"

O Lord, that I might discover
        a language responsive to Thy name!
That I might sing Your praise in
        all the earth.
How long—Thou banished Lord shall I remain
        nameless in your presence?
How long will You absent your fullness
        from our words,
Neither show Your face to the children of men?

Lord, why have You reversed the curse
        Old as the Garden from whence we came?
Why has our curse been doubled?
        As workers, unneeded to work.
By my weakness I am discarded
        because my strength has no use for me.
Infinites, small and great, are fields of exploration
        Vastnesses of infinite magnitude for our ex-
        ploitation
Yet when I consider this appetite in my smallness
Extending infinitely up and down, in and out
        Ever lengthening the frontiers of outer mystery

Ever deepening the abyss of inner spaces—
I—An infinitesimal bottleneck in the flow
        of Your ever broadening creation
Which is passed over on the outside.

My days are filled with empty longing
        Grasping frantically at the cresting waters.
My death is demanded of me every day
        Dying in the rape of fruitless objectivity
Swimming desperately like a rat
        Not built to swim so long or hard.
When will You show me how to float
        despite the horrible depths?
You have become my enemy.
        It is You only who paralyzes my strength.
I have no ground beneath my feet.
            My words are impotent to Your angry
            silence.
In my distress I cry out.
        My misery moans before Your face.
Yet I cannot pray. My hymns are impure.
            My songs are bribes and insults to Your
            name.
Such weakness sobs for Thy help,
        and the sounds of my soul sift into solitary
        silence.

Godless gods, we stand in need of God.[13]

Laments are praises in the time of God's absence, or, stated differently, in the time when his presence is hidden. Perhaps modern men are coming to know, even more radically than the psalmists who composed the poignant laments of the Psalter, that in the time of God's silence men must *wait* for God to show himself. Yet such a time is the time to "seek God's face" (see

Ps. 27:7-14) in the confidence that he will open a way into the future when there seems to be no way.

Modern man's experience of the absence of God is not irrelevant to worship: it may become the occasion for the cry "out of the depths."

4:

TASTE AND SEE
THAT THE LORD
IS GOOD!

I am reading the Psalms daily, as I have done for
years," wrote Dietrich Bonhoeffer from his prison cell
on May 15th, 1943. "I know them and love them more
than any other book in the Bible." In the same letter[1]
this martyred Christian, whose writings have had a far-
reaching influence upon the theological thinking of our
time, explains to his friends what life in prison was like,
and why he treasured laments like Psalms 3 and 70
which we considered in the last chapter. He remarks,
with a touch of humor, that he was spending his time
"reading, meditating, writing, pacing up and down my
cell—without rubbing myself sore on the walls like
a polar bear!" The main thing, he continues, is to make
use of one's powers as creatively as possible and "to
accept the limits of the situation" without "giving way
to feelings of resentment and discontent." He then expresses out of the passion of his own life the theme of
the testing of faith ("temptation") which runs throughout the Bible:

*I have never realized so clearly what the Bible and
Luther mean by spiritual trial [Anfechtung]. Quite
suddenly, for no apparent reason, whether physical
or psychological, the peace and placidity which have*

been a mainstay hitherto begin to waver, and the heart, in Jeremiah's expressive phrase, becomes that defiant and despondent thing one cannot fathom. It is like an invasion from outside, as though evil powers were trying to deprive one of life's dearest treasures. But it is a wholesome and necessary experience which helps one to a better understanding of human life. I am just trying my hand at an essay on "The feeling of time" (Zeitgefühl), a topic of peculiar interest to one like myself who is held in custody for examination. Over the door of this cell one of my predecessors here has scribbled the words "In 100 years it will all be over." That was his way of trying to overcome the feeling that time spent here is a complete blank . . . . "My time is in thy hand" (Psalm 31:15)—that is the Bible's answer. But there is also a question which the Bible asks, and which threatens to dominate the whole subject: "Lord, how long?" (Ps. 13)

Bonhoeffer knew how to pray the laments of the Psalms with a *joie de vivre*, and thus to "rejoice in the Lord" even in a situation of limitation. A friend who was with him in his last days said that Bonhoeffer "always seemed to me to diffuse an atmosphere of happiness, of joy in every smallest event in life, and of deep gratitude for the mere fact that he was alive. . . . He was one of the very few men that I have ever met to whom his God was real and close to him." [2] This faith, of course, was given to him through Jesus Christ; but it was also nourished by a rediscovery of the healthy this-worldliness of the Psalms. Psalms of lament, as we have discovered, were not the whinings of self-pity or agonized cries of utter despair. Even in situations of threat and no-exit, they expressed man's joy in the goodness of God and the goodness of the life he has given to his creatures. The psalmist responds with his whole being, including his sense of *taste:*

O taste and see that Yahweh is good!
    Happy is the man who takes refuge in him!
O fear Yahweh, you his saints,
    for those who fear him have no want!
The young lions suffer want and hunger;
    but those who seek Yahweh lack no good thing.
                    —Psalm 34:8-10

SONGS OF THANKSGIVING

Psalm 34 is usually classified as a song of thanksgiving. Before considering the form and content of this type of psalm, a word should be said about its relation to the lament on the one hand and to the hymn of praise on the other.

The lament almost invariably moves from the minor mode of complaint or penitence to the major key of thanksgiving and praise (see chap. 3). In the certainty of being heard by God, the suppliant—whether the community or the individual—anticipates God's deliverance from a situation of limitation or distress, and, in anticipation of God's gracious action, he ends his lament with a vow of praise (Pss. 7:17; 13:6; 22:22; 56:12-13; etc.). Thus the lament in Psalm 57 concludes with a song of thanksgiving:

My heart is steadfast, O God,
    my heart is steadfast!
I will sing and make melody!
    Awake, my soul!
Awake, O harp and lyre!
    I will awake the dawn!
I will give thanks to thee, O Yahweh, among the peoples;
    I will sing praises to thee among the nations.

For thy steadfast love is great to the heavens,
thy faithfulness to the clouds.
Be exalted, O God, above the heavens!
Let thy glory be over all the earth!
—Psalm 57:7-11; see also 22:23-31

This "abrupt change of mood" in the laments, to which Hermann Gunkel once called attention, is quite striking. It is doubtful whether it can be explained solely on the basis of the psalmist's inner certainty. It seems likely that the transition from sorrow to rejoicing, from lament to thanksgiving, was occasioned by something that occurred in the setting of worship within which these psalms had their place. There is evidence that at a certain point in the service a priest or prophet pronounced an "oracle" from God which assured the suppliant of grace and favor, a pronouncement which occurred also in Babylonian psalms. One such priestly assurance of help from God is probably found at the end of Psalm 55:

Cast your burden on Yahweh,
and he will sustain you;
He will never permit
the righteous to be moved.
—Psalm 55:22

Thus it was the "word of God," mediated through the cult, which modulated the tone of the suppliant's prayer from lamentation into jubilation. We may assume that in Psalm 28, for instance, just after verse 5, a minister of the cult delivered an "oracle of salvation," to which the psalmist then responded in grateful praise.

Blessed be Yahweh!
for he has heard the voice of my supplications.

Yahweh is my strength and my shield;
     in him my heart trusts;
so I am helped, and my heart exults,
     and with my song I give thanks to him.
                                    —Psalm 28:6-7

This cultic situation reminds one of Christian services of worship in which the liturgical sequence is: confession of sin and need, "words of assurance" or absolution, the Lord's Prayer, and then the response:

"O Lord, open thou my lips,
     and my mouth shall show forth thy praise."
                                    —Ps. 51:15

It can be seen, then, that a very close relationship exists between the lament and the thanksgiving. Indeed, the "song of thanksgiving" is an expanded form of the thanksgiving already present in many of the laments (Pss. 6, 13, 22, 28, 31, 55, 69, 71, 86, etc.). However, it is one thing to praise God *in anticipation* of his deliverance or on the basis of an assurance given in worship; it is another thing to praise God *in response* to an event of deliverance already experienced. It is the latter accent which characterizes the songs of thanksgiving. These songs are sung by people who in a time of distress have actually tasted the goodness of God.

Looking in another direction, the songs of thanksgiving are also closely related to hymns of praise (see chap. 5). The English reader is apt to think that all psalms which begin with an invocation to "give thanks" to God must be thanksgivings. But this is not necessarily so, for the Hebrew verb *hodah* cannot be limited to the meaning of our word "thank"; it has the wider connotation of "acknowledge, confess, proclaim," and therefore is often used in parallel with verbs meaning "praise," as in the hymn:

Enter his gates with thanksgiving,
   and his courts with praise!
   Give thanks to him, bless his name!
                    —Psalm 100:4

Therefore, we are really dealing with two ways of praising God, which can be distinguished from each other only by the form and content of the psalm. In one case, the psalmist praises God in general terms, extolling him for who he is, for his majesty as Creator, and his mighty works in history. This is the hymn. In the other case, the psalmist praises God for his action in a concrete situation of limitation and distress. This specific praise is what we mean by the song of thanksgiving. It must be admitted, however, that sometimes the line between the hymn and the song of thanksgiving cannot be drawn sharply. For instance, Psalm 136 (the "salvation history" psalm considered in chap. 2) is sometimes regarded as a hymn and sometimes as a song of thanksgiving. And Psalm 100, a hymn, is labeled "A Psalm for the thank offering [*todah*]" in the superscription.

The songs of thanksgiving, like the laments, may be divided into songs of the community and songs of the individual, though sometimes this division is somewhat uncertain, since the first personal pronoun "I" may be used in both. The community songs of thanksgiving are relatively few in number, and even these come close to being hymns. Perhaps this is because of the fact that when the community praises God for his saving power it tends to use the form of the hymn which extols him for his great deeds in history, or his majesty as Creator. The community songs of thanksgiving were used in the major festivals at the temple, especially the great Fall harvest festival of ingathering (see chap. 6).

COMMUNITY SONGS OF THANKSGIVING

   65 "Thou crownest the year with thy bounty"
         (possibly a hymn)
   67 "The earth has yielded its increase" (hymn?)
   75 "We call on thy name and recount thy won-
         drous deeds"
*107 "O give thanks to Yahweh, for he is good"
*124 "If it had not been Yahweh who was on our
         side"
 136 "It is he who remembered us in our low es-
         tate" (hymn?)
(See also the community thanksgiving in I Samuel
   2:1-10.)

The individual songs of thanksgiving, on the other hand, were composed for recitation at the temple as an expression of a person's praise to God for deliverance from a concrete distress, such as illness. In that cultic situation the individual "acknowledges" or "testifies" (the meaning of the Hebrew verb *hodah*) to the way God has acted in his own life situation. Since the word usually translated "thanksgiving" (*todah*) is the same word used for "thank offering" (Jonah 2:9; Ps. 50:14, 23), it is clear that these psalms were intended to be used in a cultic setting, that is, at a festival or other worship service at the temple. On such an occasion the individual, in the presence of the worshiping congregation (22:22; 26:12b), gave his personal testimony to God's saving deeds to the accompaniment of a ritual act (a thank offering). This is the picture given in a passage in Jeremiah which announces that in the time of restoration the voices of mirth and gladness will be heard once again, including "the voices of those who sing, as they bring thank offerings [*todah*] to the house of Yahweh":

> " '*Give thanks* [testify] *to Yahweh of hosts,*
>   *for Yahweh is good,*
>   *for his steadfast love endures for ever!*' "
> —*Jeremiah 33:11*

In this manner the individual confesses out of his own experience the faith of the whole believing community whose shared history is a witness to Yahweh's saving deeds.

INDIVIDUAL SONGS OF THANKSGIVING

18 "With the loyal thou dost show thyself loyal" (royal thanksgiving)

30 "Weeping may tarry for the night, but joy comes with the morning"

*32 "Blessed is he whose trangression is forgiven" (penitential psalm)

*34 "O taste and see that Yahweh is good!"

40 (1-11) "I waited patiently for Yahweh; he inclined to me"
(The second part of the psalm is a lament.)

66 (13-20) "Come and hear, all you who fear God"
(The first part of the psalm is a hymn.)

*92 "Thou, O Yahweh, hast made me glad by thy work"

*116 "Thou hast delivered my soul from death, my eyes from tears, and my feet from stumbling"

*118 "I shall not die, but I shall live, and recount the deeds of Yahweh" (a royal thanksgiving)

*138 "Though I walk in the midst of trouble, thou dost preserve my life"

(See also the individual thanksgivings in Isaiah 38:9-
20 and Jonah 2:2-9.)

Notice that in the above list two of the psalms are
designated as royal thanksgivings. In these the king
("the Anointed One"—in Hebrew, the word equivalent
to "messiah") speaks not just as an individual, but as
the representative of the people. This is the case in
Psalm 118 (Luther's favorite psalm)—a psalm that is
often quoted in the New Testament. The king's song of
thanksgiving in verses 5-21 is offered in a cultic situation,
as evidenced by the request for admission through the
temple gates so that he may give thanks (vs. 19), the
choral blessing from the temple (vs. 26), and the solemn
festal procession to the altar (vs. 27). Thus the worshiping community takes part in the thanksgiving and
identifies itself with the king's testimony to the saving
power of God. It is not surprising that a psalm which
belonged so deeply to Israel's worship was eventually
referred to *the* Anointed One (Messiah), as happens in
the New Testament. In the larger context of the Christian Bible the central image of this psalm—the stone,
rejected by the builders, which has become the chief
cornerstone (vss. 22-25)—is identified with Jesus Christ,
the "king," whom God has exalted from rejection and
humiliation to a crucial place of honor in the divine
purpose (Matt. 21:42; Acts 4:11; I Peter 2:7). And since
in every Christian worship service the community gives
praise and thanks for God's victory in Christ, a victory
in which men of faith may participate, it is appropriate
to say on "the Lord's Day" (Sunday, the day of Resurrection):

This is the day which Yahweh has made;
let us rejoice and be glad in it.
                    —Psalm 118:24

The song of thanksgiving is cast in a form which, allowing for variations, may be traced quite clearly in the songs of the individual.

1. Introduction

   The worshiper announces his intention to give thanks to God. This address, which may be short or omitted altogether, is usually made to Yahweh in the second person ("thou"), as in Psalm 30, for example.

2. Main Section: narration of the psalmist's experience
   (a) Portrayal of the distress in which he had found himself
   (b) His cry to God for help
   (c) The deliverance

3. Conclusion

   The worshiper again testifies to Yahweh's gracious act. A prayer for future help, or a confession that Yahweh is gracious, or some other formulation may be added.

As an example to guide in the study of the psalms marked with an asterisk in the above list, let us consider the psalm of thanksgiving which has been inserted into the story of Jonah. We say "inserted" because the psalm is obviously out of place in its present context. In the belly of a fish a cry for help (that is, a lament) would be appropriate, but not a thanksgiving for deliverance already experienced!

1. Introduction: a summary of the testimony of the psalmist (Jonah 2:2)

   "I called to Yahweh, out of my distress,
   and he answered me;

out of the belly of Sheol I cried,
and thou didst hear my voice."

2. Main Section:
   (a) Portrayal of affliction (Jonah 2:3-6*a*)
   "For thou didst cast me into the deep,
   into the heart of the seas,
   and the flood was round about me;
   all thy waves and thy billows
   passed over me.
   Then I said, 'I am cast out
   from thy presence;
   how shall I again look
   upon thy holy temple?'
   The waters closed in over me,
   the deep was round about me;
   weeds were wrapped about my head
   at the roots of the mountains.
   I went down to the land
   whose bars closed upon me for ever."

   (b) Petition for help (Jonah 2:6*b*-7)
   "Yet thou didst bring up my life from the Pit,
   O Yahweh my God.
   When my soul fainted within me,
   I remembered Yahweh;
   and my prayer came to thee,
   into thy holy temple."

   (c) Deliverance (this motif is found as a preface
   to the petition)
   ["Yet thou didst bring up my life from the Pit,
   O Yahweh, my God."]

3. Conclusion: acknowledgment of God's gracious
   act and the promise to present a thank offering
   (Jonah 2:8-9)

"Those who pay regard to vain idols
forsake their true loyalty.
But I with the voice of thanksgiving
will sacrifice to thee;
what I have vowed I will pay.
Deliverance belongs to Yahweh!"

We shall return to the psalmist's portrayal of the
threat of death as a descent into "hell" (Sheol). Here,
however, a special word should be said about the *todah*
—the offering which the worshiper vows to present in
grateful acknowledgment of God's help. The same thing
is found in Psalm 116. After an introduction (vss. 1-2),
and a portrayal of his experience of deliverance from
distress (vss. 3-11), the worshiper vows to offer "the
sacrifice of thanksgiving" at the temple (vss. 12-19).

What shall I render to Yahweh
for all his bounty to me?
I will lift up the cup of salvation
and call on the name of Yahweh,
I will pay my vows to Yahweh
in the presence of all his people.
—Psalm 116:12-14

This picture of a votive offering in the form of lifting
"the cup of salvation" may be only a metaphor here;
but at one time it was a cultic act, on which archaeology
has shed some light. Otto Eissfeldt draws our attention
to a Phoenician votive stele (upright stone) from the
fifth century B.C. belonging to Yehawmilk, king of
Byblos. The text is addressed to the goddess Ba'alat,
the female counterpart of the great storm-god Baal:

Yehawmilk, king of Byblos, to my lady, Ba'alat of
Byblos. For when I cried to my lady, Ba'alat of Byblos,
then she heard me and showed me favour.

Interestingly, there is a picture above the inscription which shows the king standing before the goddess, who is seated on her throne. In his hand he holds a libation cup which he lifts up to her. Thus the acknowledgment of thanks and the thank offering are combined in this votive stele, precisely as they are combined in the Psalms.³ Here again we have evidence that Israelite worship was influenced by ancient forms of worship, though these forms were transformed to express Israel's distinctive faith.

It is noteworthy that these songs of thanksgiving retained their basic form even after they became detached from their original cultic setting and became "spiritual songs." This is evidenced in the songs of thanksgiving found among the Dead Sea scriptures, to which we referred previously (chapter 1). These songs characteristically begin with the testimony "I thank thee"; then follows an address to the deity; and this in turn is followed by a clause, introduced by the motive word *ki* (usually translated "for," "that") which gives the specific reason for offering thanks to God. This thanksgiving genre, which was current in the Judaism out of which Christianity emerged, came to be prominent in the New Testament "eucharistic" tradition. (Eucharist comes from a Greek verb meaning "thank." ⁴) The Epistle to the Ephesians contains this advice to the Christian community: "Be filled with the Spirit, addressing one another in psalms and hymns and spiritual songs, singing and making melody to the Lord with all your heart, always and for everything giving thanks in the name of our Lord Jesus Christ to God the Father" (Ephesians 5:18*b*-20).

DELIVERANCE FROM THE POWER OF DEATH

Attention has been called to the fact that one of the so-called penitential psalms, Psalm 32, is a song of thanksgiving, not a lament. In this psalm the suppliant bears testimony to his deliverance from guilt, which, before his confession of sin to God, worked as a destructive power within the personality.

When I declared not my sin, my body wasted away
    through my groaning all day long.
For day and night thy hand was heavy upon me;
    my strength was dried up as by the heat of summer.

I acknowledged my sin to thee,
    and I did not hide my iniquity;
I said, "I will confess my transgressions to Yahweh";
    then thou didst forgive the guilt of my sin.
—Psalm 32:3-5

It seems that here sin has something of the destructive power of death (compare Paul's statement, "the sting of death is sin" in I Cor. 15:56). This psalm, then, provides a transition to other individual songs of thanksgiving which deal primarily with deliverance from the power of death.

It is likely that a number of the individual songs of thanksgiving were composed for, or at least usable in, the situation described in Isaiah 38, which is usually known by the obscure reference to the "miraculous" retreat of the sun's shadow. The story goes (Isa. 38:1-8) that King Hezekiah was suffering a "sickness unto death." On the point of death, he raised a lament which in content is like the laments we have considered. Hezekiah "wept bitterly":

"Remember now, O Yahweh, I beseech thee, how I have walked before thee in faithfulness and with a whole heart, and have done what is good in thy sight."
—Isaiah 38:2-3

In response to his lament the prophet Isaiah delivered an "oracle of salvation," or words of assurance (vss. 4ff.). And, as in actual cultic practice, there follows a song (vss. 9-20), traditionally ascribed to Hezekiah, for the use of an individual giving thanks to God at the temple after deliverance from affliction. In form this psalm is like others that we have listed in the category of individual thanksgivings (e.g., Psalm 32 or Jonah 2:2-9). On the surface it seems that such psalms were simply used to thank God for recovery from illness.

However, when one reads the thanksgivings in the Psalter, especially in connection with the individual laments, he is struck by their "dynamic" view of death. The understanding of death is not what we are accustomed to in our Western culture. The prevalent view today is that death is a biological event which occurs when the heart stops beating and consciousness goes out like a light. Death, according to this generally accepted notion, comes *at the end of life*. This terminus is often recognized with a mixture of melancholy and sentimentalism in the ritual of the funeral service—especially those which are taken out of the context of the worshiping congregation and handed over to the funeral parlors.

The Psalms are filled with an awareness of the brevity and frailty of human life (Pss. 90:3-10; 103:14-16). But what strikes us most is the psalmists' view that death works its power in us *now*, during our historical experience. According to the Israelite view, death brings about "a decrease in the vitality of the individual." [5] Death's power is felt in the midst of life to the degree that one experiences any weakening of his powers through illness, handicap, imprisonment, attack from enemies, or advancing old age. Any threat to a person's welfare (Hebrew: *shalom*, peace or well-being), that is, to his freedom to be and to participate in the covenant community, is understood to be an invasion of the empire of death into the historical arena.

This reference to death's imperialism—its territorial ambition to encroach into "the land of the living"—deserves further consideration. The psalmists' portrayals of the threat of death are couched in a pictorial (mythical) language expressive of a way of thinking which, at first glance, seems alien to our experience. Israel inherited a picture of the universe which depicted man's world as surrounded on every hand by "the waters of chaos" which, at the time of creation, the Creator subdued and pushed back in order to give man historical space in which to live and to perform his God-given task (Gen. 1:1-2:4a). The earth is portrayed as a kind of island, suspended over the waters of the "deep," within which is located Sheol, the kingdom of death; and beyond the great blue dome overhead are the waters of the heavenly ocean which, unless held back by the protective barrier of the firmament, would flood the world with chaos (as almost happened, according to the Flood Story). It is wrong to convert this pictorial view into a pre-scientific "three-storied conception of the universe," as has happened in some modern discussions of the Bible. In the Psalms this language is used religiously or poetically to express man's awareness that on all sides the historical world is threatened by powers of chaos which, were they not held back by the Creator, would engulf man and reduce existence to meaningless confusion.

This enables us to understand the many references in the Psalter to coming into deep waters, to the engulfing waves and billows, or to the "descent into hell" (Sheol, the Pit, Abaddon ["the place of destruction"]). In the psalm of Jonah, as we have noticed, the suppliant cries to Yahweh "out of the depths." Using poetic imagery he says that he has been "cast into the deep," that the

waves and billows have gone over him, and that he has
plunged, like a drowning man, down to the very roots
of the mountains. The same imagery is found in the
royal thanksgiving, Psalm 18 (see vss. 4-6). In the
latter psalm, however, the divine rescue is vividly described in terms of mythical language appropriated
from the Canaanites. Yahweh is portrayed as the Divine
Warrior who, in an awe-inspiring theophany of thunderstorm (vss. 7-15; cf. Ps. 29:3-9), comes to battle with
the waters of chaos (the mythical sea) and drives them
back to their place.

He reached from on high, he took me,
    he drew me out of many waters,
He delivered me from my strong enemy,
    and from those who hated me;
    for they were too mighty for me.
They came upon me in the day of my calamity;
    but Yahweh was my stay.
He brought me forth into a broad place;
    he delivered me, because he delighted in me.
                —Psalm 18:16-19

Here we see how the historical enemies of the king are
associated with the powers of chaos which threaten
God's creation (cf., also, Ps. 144:1-11).[6]

In the Canaanite mythology which has profoundly influenced these portrayals, Death (*Mot*) was regarded as
a god in his own right—the powerful king of the under-
world. Acording to Ugaritic mythological literature from
about 1400 B.C., Mot seeks to extend his kingdom over
the earth and thereby challenges the authority of 'El,
the Father of the gods. However, the youthful storm
god, known as Aleyn Baal, takes up the challenge and
wins a great victory over Mot, whereupon Baal is acclaimed as King. The conquest of death is not decisive,

however; it has to be repeated every year as the cycle of the seasons moves from the barrenness of winter to the renewal of fertility in the spring, from death to resurrection. The Israelite faith, in confrontation with the Baal religion which dominated Canaan, repudiated the view that the meaning of man's existence is given in the rhythms of nature. It proclaimed, rather, God's historical actions in decisive, non-recurring events (chiefly the Exodus) which called the people Israel into being and guided them in their historical journey. However, Israel appropriated the old mythical language and reinterpreted it to express historical experiences of threat and limitation which seemed to call into question the sovereignty of God. In the Psalms death is a power (though no longer a deity) that reaches out greedily to lay hold of the living, a deposed king whose shadowy kingdom encroaches upon man's historical world, an enemy that stands in opposition to the purpose of God. The psalmists testify that it is only God who can save men from death's power.[7]

In the Psalms this struggle against the encroachment of death into man's historical world is never resolved by a clear and unambiguous expression of belief in a future life. Indeed, when we read in English translation the affirmation, "Thou hast delivered my soul from death" (Ps. 116:8), we must guard against reading into the word "soul" the notion of an element within the body which by nature is deathless and indestructible. The Greek doctrine of the "immortality" (deathlessness) of the soul is not attested in the Old Testament, or for that matter, even in the New Testament. Only God is essentially immortal (I Tim. 6:16); man is a mortal who, as the story in Genesis 2 puts it, is made "from the ground and returns to the ground." The word translated "soul" (Hebrew: *nefesh*) means "self, person" as a psychosomatic unity. If the self has a future, as indeed the New Testament emphatically proclaims, God will, in a marvelous way, past our comprehension, raise it and give it a new form of existence. The "resurrection of the body" (that is, the self) is attested in Paul's great discussion in I Corinthians 15, and of course is basic to the church's creedal affirmation: "I believe in the resurrection of the body [not "flesh"] and the life everlasting." This Christian view, however, is not found in the Psalter.

What, then, is the concern of the psalmists when they give thanks to Yahweh for delivering them from the power of death? Certainly they are not just glad to regain physical health, or to add more years to their life, or to enhance the life they now enjoy with greater comfort or security. That is a modern conception of life, whose emptiness is eventually disclosed. According to Israel's way of thinking, life is missed when men do not *choose* it (see Deut. 30:15-20 with its alternative: "See, I have set before you life and death . . . therefore choose life!"). Moreover, the life of the "righteous" is eroded in vitality when death works its power. As Christoph Barth observes, what the psalmists pray for in laments, or thank God for in thanksgiving, is "the restoration of life that they have lost" or "its radical *renewal* through true life"—that is, the life that is given to man in his relationship to God in the covenant community.[8] For the psalmists the tragedy of death is that it transposes people into another, non-historical realm where they can no longer praise God (Ps. 88:10-12). When a person has lost the capacity for wonder and no longer praises God, he is dead. On the other hand, when a person is restored to a meaningful place within the worshiping community, when his relationship to God and his fellow man is renewed, then he begins to live again and to sing praises. Then he can declare that it is God who revives his whole *nefesh* or being (Ps. 23:3).

A robust this-worldliness thus characterized Israel's faith. The notion that this world is only a preparation for the next, or that earthly experience is lower and therefore inferior to some higher realm of reality, is completely alien to the Old Testament. This view, which still prevails in much Christian thinking, originated under the influence of Hellenistic philosophies which drew a sharp distinction between the eternal realm of unchanging Reality and the temporal realm of change, flux, and contingency, where eternal truth is, at best, only intimated in a shadowy form. The psalms, however, bear witness to the fundamental goodness of life as God has given it to us. All of the senses—sight, hearing, taste, touch, and smell—are to be employed in the enjoyment of life to the full, in whatever time is given. To be sure, this love of life is not a shallow sense of happiness, such as modern man craves with the gadgets and benefits afforded by science and technology. There is, as we have noted repeatedly, a minor strain of grief, anxiety, and even God-forsakenness which runs through life's experiences; but these are transmuted into praise by people who expect to see "the goodness of Yahweh in the land of the living" (Ps. 27:13). The psalmists insist that the man who lives in relationship to God is "blessed" (or "happy"). For in faith such a man knows, again and again, that "God's Yes is spoken in the midst of life" (Westermann).

It is therefore highly appropriate that the Christian church, which has heard God's Yes pronounced decisively in Jesus Christ, should find its faith nourished by the Psalms of the Old Testament. This point was appreciated profoundly by Dietrich Bonhoeffer, to whom we referred in the beginning of this chapter and whom we now hear again at the end. In an Advent meditation he wrote:

My thoughts and feelings seem to be getting more and more like the Old Testament, and no wonder, I have been reading it much more than the New for the last few months. It is only when one knows the ineffability of the Name of God that one can utter the name of Jesus Christ. It is only when one loves life and the world so much that without them everything would be gone, that one can believe in the resurrection and a new world. It is only when one submits to the law that one can speak of grace, and only when one sees the anger and wrath of God hanging like grim realities over the head of one's enemies that one can know something of what it means to love them and forgive them. I don't think it is Christian to want to get to the New Testament too soon and too directly.[9]

There is much truth in this. If one bypasses the Psalms, with their taste for the goodness of life, he is apt to miss the fullness of the New Testament gospel which announces that Jesus Christ came that men might have life and have it abundantly.

5:

HOW MAJESTIC
IS THY NAME
IN ALL THE EARTH!

"We must put away all thoughts of paper and ink," wrote Hermann Gunkel in a lecture on "The Religion of the Psalms," "and look on the Psalms as having their source in the life of the people." [1] It is this life-centered approach which we have been following in the foregoing discussion as we have attempted to understand the place of psalm-singing in the worship of Israel.

Israel's praise of God, we have seen, was evoked in the first instance not by a general religious awareness of God's wisdom and power manifest in the broad expanse of creation and the history of mankind but, rather, by the experience of his active presence and power in the life-situation of Israel, his people. Yahweh's intervention into the historical plight of a band of slaves— victims of the Egyptian Pharaoh who was the mightiest emperor of the day—had the wonderful result of creating a people "out of nothing" and opening a way into the future. As we read in the story of the call of Moses, Yahweh "heard" the cry of his people under oppression, he "knew" their sufferings, and he "came down" to deliver them and to bring them into "a good and broad land, a land flowing with milk and honey" (Ex. 3:7-8).

Hence Israel's earliest songs, as in the case of the Song of Miriam (Ex. 15:21), were jubilant cries of praise in response to the God who had acted with saving power.

Since Israel's faith was rooted in life-situations before it was written down with "paper and ink," it is appropriate that we have turned initially to the psalms which express the cry to God out of concrete distress (the laments) and the praise to God for a particular act of deliverance just experienced (songs of thanksgiving). However, these songs "out of the depths" inevitably lead in the direction of *hymns* which praise God in general terms for the majesty of his being—for his greatness and goodness as Creator and Lord of history. The lament found in Psalm 102, for instance, contains hymnic elements (vss. 12-22, 25-28). And Psalm 107, a thanksgiving on behalf of various groups—those who had traveled safely in the desert, those delivered from prison, those healed from sickness, and those who voyaged safely on storm-tossed ships—appropriately concludes with a hymn of praise to God for his providential care (vss. 33-43).

Psalm 98 is an excellent illustration of how life-situational praise of God, the "Vindicator" of Israel, leads to the singing of a "new song" in which all the inhabitants of the earth and even the vast realms of nature are summoned to worship.

O sing to Yahweh a new song,
>   for he has done marvelous things!
His right hand and his holy arm
>   have gotten him victory.
Yahweh has made known his victory,
>   he has revealed his vindication in the sight of the
>   nations.
He has remembered his steadfast love and faithfulness
>   to the house of Israel.

**All the ends of the earth have seen
the victory of our God.**

—Psalm 98:1-3

In this hymn Israel's horizon expands from the praise of "our God"—the God who revealed himself dynamically in Israel's historical experience—to general or "descriptive" praise of the God who is Creator and Lord of the whole earth.

THE FORM AND SETTING OF THE HYMN

The hymn (Hebrew, *tehilla*) is concisely defined as "the song which extols the glory and greatness of Yahweh as it is revealed in nature and history, and particularly in Israel's history."[2] This definition rightly indicates that Israelite hymns placed particular stress upon Yahweh's active involvement in the life-story of Israel. In the so-called salvation-history psalms (chap. 2), the "mighty deeds" of Yahweh were retold didactically "so that the next generation might know them" (Ps. 78:1-8); and during the great festivals Yahweh's actions probably were re-enacted in a ritual drama so that worshipers might "see" what God had done for Israel and thereby experience directly the power and meaning of the salvation history (compare Pss. 66:5, 6; 46:8).[3] But it is equally true that the hymns of Israel have a universal and cosmic dimension. In the temple of Jerusalem, worshipers confessed that the "glory" (radiance) of Yahweh which filled the sanctuary when he was present to his worshiping people also suffused the whole universe. This is evident from the story of Isaiah's call (Isa. 6) where, in the prophet's vision, the Jerusalem temple seems to be only a copy of the heavenly temple in which Yahweh is enthroned as *the* King. The hymn that the prophet hears resounding in the heavenly temple is undoubtedly the echo of one that was sung in the earthly sanctuary in Jerusalem:

> *Holy, holy, holy is the Lord of hosts;*
> *the whole earth is full of his glory.*
> —*Isaiah 6:3*

The structure of the hymn is given in its simplest form in the Song of Miriam (Ex. 15:21), which begins with an imperative summons to praise and continues with an announcement of the motive for praise (introduced by the motive word, *ki*). This form is found also in the shortest psalm of the Psalter, Psalm 117:

A. *Praise Yahweh, all nations!*
   Extol him, all peoples!
B. *For [ki] great is his steadfast love toward us;*
   and the faithfulness of Yahweh endures
   for ever.
C. *Praise Yahweh!* [4]

Here is a psalm which is purposefully short and simple, as Luther once remarked, so that anyone can grasp its meaning. The simplicity of the content is matched by the clarity of its form.

As the above outline indicates, the hymn contains the following elements:

A. Introduction: call to worship
   This is usually an imperative, in the second person plural. It can be a "bidding" formula such as "O come, let us sing . . ." (95:1-2) or a summons addressed to the psalmist's *self*, such as "Bless [praise] Yahweh, O my soul . . ." (Ps. 103:1). The note struck in the introduction may be repeated in the psalm (e.g., 95:6) or even expanded to great length (as in Ps. 148).

B. Main Section: the motive for praise

In many cases the transition to the motive for praise is introduced by "for" (Hebrew: *ki*), as in Ps. 33:4 or 95:3 and 7. This is sometimes varied by using "who" clauses, as in Ps. 103:3-5, or by introducing long passages which portray God's majesty as displayed in history or creation (e.g., Ps. 104:5-30).

C. Recapitulation

Often the psalm concludes with a renewed summons to praise, thus echoing the note struck at the beginning.

In the genre of the hymn the most important element is the main section which gives the ground or motive for praise. A typical example is this hymnic outburst in the poetry of Second Isaiah:

Break forth together into singing,
you waste places of Jerusalem;
for [ki] Yahweh has comforted his people,
he has redeemed Jerusalem.
Yahweh has bared his holy arm
before the eyes of all the nations;
and all the ends of the earth shall see
the salvation of our God.
—Isaiah 52:9-10

[Compare also the hymnic fragment in Isaiah 44:23.]

Hymns with this form were undoubtedly used on a variety of worship occasions in the temple, much as general hymns of praise in modern hymnbooks are used in our regular services of worship. Other hymns seem to have been used for special festal occasions, corresponding to special music used in our churches at Christmas, Thanksgiving, or Easter. A number of hymns, the so-called psalms of Yahweh's enthronement, were probably used in connection with the great festival held in Jerusalem in the autumn (New Year's Festival). These "enthronement psalms," along with psalms celebrating the Davidic kingship and the choice of Zion, will be considered in chapter 6.

In the following outline the hymns of general praise are grouped according to three thematic categories, though the assignment of particular psalms is somewhat arbitrary in the second and third categories. Notice that many of these hymns extol God in the third person (he), in contrast to the psalms of thanksgiving which usually address God in the second person (you).

HYMNS TO THE CREATOR OF THE UNIVERSE
("CREATION PSALMS")

*8 "How majestic is thy name in all the earth!"
*19 (1-6) "The heavens are telling the glory of God" (The second part of the psalm is a meditation on the Law of Yahweh.)
*104 "O Yahweh, how manifold are thy works!"
*148 "His glory is above earth and heaven"

HYMNS TO THE GOD WHO CREATED AND CHOSE ISRAEL

66 (1-12) " 'How terrible [awe-inspiring] are thy deeds!' " (The second part of the psalm is an individual thanksgiving.)
*100 "It is he that made us, and we are his"
111 "He has caused his wonderful works to be remembered"
114 "When Israel went forth from Egypt"
149 "Let Israel be glad in his Maker"

[See also the hymns in Ex. 15:1-18, Habakkuk 3:2-19, and the song in Deuteronomy
32:1-43.]

HYMNS TO THE CREATOR AS THE LORD OF HISTORY

*33 "The earth is full of the steadfast love of Yah-
weh"
*103 "Bless Yahweh, O my soul, and forget not all
his benefits"
113 "From the rising of the sun to its setting the
name of Yahweh is to be praised!"
117 "Praise Yahweh, all nations!"
*145 "All thy works shall give thanks to [praise]
thee, O Yahweh"
[Note that the verb here, which is parallel
to "bless," should be translated "praise"
or "testify to."]
*146 "I will praise Yahweh as long as I live"
*147 "Great is our Lord, and abundant in power"

Psalm 150 is not included in the above outline because,
as we have noted previously, it is a doxology which
rounds off the whole Psalter. Nevertheless, it is particularly interesting in this context because it calls upon a
whole orchestra of instruments, including trumpet, lute,
harp, timbrel, strings, pipe, and cymbals, to join in praising Yahweh. This psalm clearly indicates that Israel's
praise was not a quiet meditation but rather the making
of a "joyful noise" to Yahweh "with timbrel and dance"
(vs. 4; cf. Pss. 33:2-3; 149:3). Such a psalm is reminis-
cent of the earliest days when Miriam praised Yahweh
to the accompaniment of "timbrels and dancing" (Ex.
15:20-21). Here again we notice that worship, being the
response of the whole being to God's overture, may take
the form of bodily movement, set to the rhythms of

music and dance. This does not necessarily suggest the frenzied excitement of prophetic groups who used music, drugs, and dancing to stimulate religious ecstasy (cf. I Sam. 10:5-6, 9-13). It is perhaps more like the Greek dramas in which the chorus, through singing and dancing, expressed the people's involvement in the drama.

THE NAME OF GOD

The hymn was not unique with Israel. Thanks to archaeological research we now have at our disposal a large treasury of hymns from Israel's neighbors: hymns to Amon-Re, to Ishtar, to Marduk, and to other gods and goddesses worshiped by the Egyptians, Sumerians, Babylonians, Hittites, and Canaanites.[5] What is unique about Israel's hymns is that they are praises of *Yahweh, the God of Israel*. This praise found expression in a new kind of speech to God. In some respects this new speech carried over idioms of the past: for instance, the expression "a great King above all gods" (Ps. 95:3) is traditional language, based on the ancient picture of the King who presides over the heavenly council, "the assembly of the holy ones" (Ps. 89:5-6; cf. I Kings 22:19; Job 1:6). What is more important here is that Israel praised Yahweh by pouring a completely *new content* into the ancient form of the hymn. Israel's hymn is appropriately called a "new song" (Pss. 96:1; 98:1).

In chapter 1, when introductory matters pertaining to the Psalter were under consideration, we noticed that one collection of psalms stands apart because of its use of the general term for deity, *'Elohim* (God), in preference to the special name *Yahweh* (Lord). This Elohistic Psalter (Pss. 42-83) was compiled in a circle which, for some reason not completely clear to us, shunned the use of the name Yahweh. This peculiarity is so striking that it focuses attention sharply on the fact that the Psalter as a whole ascribes praise to *Yahweh*. When Elijah challenged the people at Mount Carmel, "If Yahweh is God, follow him; but if Baal, then follow him" (I Kings 18: 21), none answered; but the answer of the psalmists would have been immediate and clear: "Know that *Yahweh* is God!" (Ps. 100:3); "Bless Yahweh, O my soul; and all that is within me, bless his holy name!" (Ps. 103:1). Since Israelite faith was at no stage a tolerant polytheism, or even a predilection for one supreme God out of many, the stress upon the divine name deserves attention. Usually Christian worshipers skip lightly over this matter when reciting the words of the Lord's Prayer: "Hallowed be thy name."

In the ancient Israelite world, as in some societies today, the question of the name was a supremely important issue—one which could not have been challenged, as it was in Shakespeare's tragedy, with the innocent query, "What's in a name?" (*Romeo and Juliet*, act 2, scene 2). Among the Israelites the name was understood to be the expression of the nature or identity of a person.[6] Although in our society names have tended to become labels, we can still appreciate the Israelite view, at least imaginatively. Nothing is more pathetic than the person who, because of amnesia, cannot remember his own name, that is, who he is. And nothing is more shocking than the report that prisoners in concentration camps were divested of their personal names and given numbers. A person's name is the expression of his identity, an identity which is bound up essentially with his personal history.

From this standpoint we may begin to understand the Israelite concern to know the name of God. God's name is the aspect of his being that is turned graciously toward his people. His name is his identity which is bound up with events in which he has displayed his faithfulness and steadfast love. Therefore it is characteristic for Israel to refer to God in "who-clauses": "I am Yahweh your God, who brought you out of the land of Egypt, out of the house of bondage" (Ex. 20:2). An ancient formula for the act of worship is "to call upon the name of Yahweh" (Gen. 4:26b). In the existential crises of life, the question "*Who* is our God?" is of supreme importance.

Living as we do in an increasingly cosmopolitan world, this Israelite zeal to know and honor God's name may sometimes seem harsh, if not anachronistic. There is considerable appeal for many in the mystical religions of the East which declare that the divine is Unnameable. The naming of God, it is said, is a limitation which reduces God to the world of man's relative distinctions, to man's history; therefore all divine names (Allah, Yahweh, Brahma, Christ, etc.) point beyond to a Reality that is nameless. Yet it is precisely God's turning toward man —his entrance into the human situation to disclose who he is and who man is—which is the heart of the biblical story. This momentous event is reported in the third chapter of Exodus in connection with the episode of "the burning bush." Moses attempts to sidestep his commission as God's spokesman by protesting that, if he goes back to his kinsmen in Egypt and reports a visitation from God, they will want to know, "What is his name?" (Ex. 3:13). At first the answer is given in somewhat enigmatic terms, "*I Will Be Who I Will Be*"—a phrase which in the Hebrew is a wordplay on the name "Yahweh." [7] Apparently the Israelite narrator wants to say that God does not give his name lightly, lest men take it in vain by attempting to manipulate and control God for their own purposes. But, taking this risk, God tells Moses to say to the Israelites that he has been sent by *Yahweh*, the God of their fathers: "this is my name for ever, and thus I am to be remembered throughout all generations" (Ex. 3:15). In this way God graciously condescends to make himself known to Israel and to be with his people on their historical journey.

Because God turns personally toward his people, they may have access to him in worship and put their trust in him personally. A psalmist says, "Those who know thy name put their trust in thee" (Ps. 9:10). It is impossible to understand the faith of the Psalms apart from Israel's witness that God has chosen to reveal *himself*—who he is—in Israel's history (see Ps. 76:1), and through this history to the whole world. It is surely not accidental that, with the exception of the Elohistic Psalter, Israel hallows the name of God in worship. Even in the case of these Elohistic psalms, we must assume that before they were edited in this manner the name of the God of Israel was invoked.

THE HEAVENS ARE TELLING THE GLORY OF GOD

The question is: How do men know who God is, that is, in what manner is his Name revealed? This question has often been discussed on the basis of Psalm 19, one of the "creation psalms." Actually this psalm is composed of two distinct pieces: the first (vss. 1-6) is an old song which praises the God whose "glory" (radiance) is displayed in the heavens; the second part (vss. 7-14) is a meditation on the *torah* (Law) in which Yahweh, the God known in Israel's history, has disclosed his will. It is worth considering whether these two parts belong together.

In the first part of the psalm (designated Psalm 19A), the special Name of God, Yahweh, is not employed. Rather, Psalm 19A seems to be an old song which praises *'El* (translated "God" in vs. 1), the ancient Semitic title for the Father of the Gods. The psalmist affirms that the phenomena of the heavens, especially the sun, are constantly proclaiming the glory of *'El* in a great anthem of praise, inaudible to human ears.

The heavens are telling the glory of God ['El];
>and the firmament proclaims his handiwork.
Day to day pours forth speech,
>and night to night declares knowledge.
>>—Psalm 19:1-2

Night and day—like antiphonal choirs—take up the ceaseless strains of the anthem of praise. Yet while this anthem is sung in the universal language of nature, it is a *silent* testimony which is not clearly understandable to man. This seems to be emphasized in the next lines:

There is no speech, nor are there words;
>their voice is not heard;
yet their voice [perhaps "measuring-line"] goes out through
>>all the earth,
>and their words to the end of the world.
>>—Psalm 19:3-4*b*

The psalmist then draws upon the pagan myth of the sun god who at night has his abode in the mythical "Sea," where he rests in the arms of his beloved, and at dawn emerges from his bridal chamber with youthful vigor and radiant splendor.

In them [perhaps "In the sea"] he has set a tent for the sun,
>which comes forth like a bridegroom leaving his
>>chamber,
>and like a strong man runs its course with joy.
Its rising is from the end of the heavens,
>and its circuit to the end of them;
>and there is nothing hid from its heat.
>>—Psalm 19:4*c*-6

In these verses man's elemental response to nature, as expressed in the myths of the ancient world, is reinterpreted in the light of faith in the God who is not a power of nature (the deified Sun or Moon) but is the Creator who transcends nature. The light which suffuses the universe is more than the radiance of the sun: it is the "glory" of deity—the shining light which both reveals and hides God's being (Isa. 6:1-3; Ezek. 1-3).

It is questionable whether the psalmist intends to say that God reveals *himself* in nature. The works of creation disclose God's "glory" and his "handiwork," but not his will or his gracious concern for man. There is a kind of knowledge of God available in nature, as Paul points out in Romans 1:19-20 (knowledge of "God's eternal power and deity"), but it is not saving knowledge which answers the psalmist's question, "What is man that thou art mindful of him?" (Ps. 8:4).

The second part of the psalm (Psalm 19B), as we have noted, is an independent literary piece. Probably it was composed much later than the first part. Yet the editorial combination of the psalms was hardly accidental. An Old Testament theologian, Gerhard von Rad, maintains that the second part was meant to be a supplement to and correction of the old hymn which draws upon mythical ideas found in the religions of the ancient world. Psalm 19B, he says, expresses "a certain doubt" that man knows God on the basis of the works of the creation. The combination of the two songs—one on the creation and the other on the *torah* (Law)—is a theological testimony that "Israel's praise is directed to Yahweh's historical self-revelation given peculiarly to herself." [8] In other words, the psalm in its combined form is not concerned merely with *'El* (deity); rather, it is based on the conviction that God has broken through the silences of nature, disclosing who he is (his Name), and speaking in the history of his people.

This understanding of Psalm 19 is expressed in the

lines of a well-known hymn by Isaac Watts (1674-1748):

> *The heavens declare thy glory, Lord;*
> *In every star thy wisdom shines;*
> *But when our eyes behold thy Word,*
> *We read thy name in fairer lines.*[9]

For the man of faith, nature does bear impressive witness to the glory of God, but only because, first of all, in the history remembered and actualized by the believing community, "we read [his] name in fairer lines."

THE LORD OF HISTORY AND CREATION

In order to understand Israel's testimony that Yahweh is Creator, as in the so-called creation psalms and in references scattered throughout the Psalter (e.g., 33:6-9; 90:2; 96:5; 124:8; 146:6), it is important to turn to those psalms which understand creation in relation to history, particularly those psalms which praise Yahweh as "Israel's Maker." This view of creation as a historical event—the bringing into existence and preservation of a people—is expressed, at least implicitly, in the salvation history psalms which we have considered earlier. In other psalms, as in the "Old Hundredth," the view is explicit.

Know that Yahweh is God!
It is he that made us, and we are his;
we are his people, and the sheep of his pasture.
—Psalm 100:2

Here the affirmation, "God is our creator," has its counterpart in the confession "we are his" (probably the correct reading of the Hebrew at this point). To confess faith in Yahweh as the creator of a people is to acknowledge absolute dependence upon him. The affirmation "we are his" becomes, by extension, the confession that the whole earth belongs to him and is dependent upon him for its being and meaning. Thus we read at the beginning of Psalm 24:

> **The earth is Yahweh's and the fulness thereof,**
> > **the world and those who dwell therein;**
> **for he has founded it upon the seas,**
> > **and established it upon the rivers.**
> > > **—Psalm 24:1-2**

This view of the creation as wholly and solely dependent upon Yahweh moment by moment is expressed magnificently in Psalm 104—a psalm which was influenced by Egyptian hymnology.[10]

Israel's praise, then, is not directed to "deity" in general but to the God who has made himself known in judgment and in mercy in Israel's peculiar historical experience. The people who know God's name perceive his signature in the whole earth and in the starry cosmos. Thus the magnificent creation Psalm 8 begins and ends —in the characteristic form of a hymn—with an invocation to Yahweh:

> **O Yahweh, our Lord,**
> > **how majestic is thy name in all the earth!**
> > > **—Psalm 8:1, 9**

The psalmist proclaims with the worshiping community that the God whose word is *audible* in Israel's history ("our Lord") is the God whose "glory" is *visible* in heaven and earth. The motive for praise is introduced in verse 3 with the word *ki* (translated here as "when"), and is developed in a passage in which the psalmist affirms that to know God's name is to live in the wonder of his gracious turning toward man. Not only does Yahweh show concern for his transient creature, man, but he has exalted him to a position of proximity to the divine realm: just "a little less than 'Elohim ["God" or probably, "angels"]." [11]

When [ki] I look at thy heavens, the work of thy fingers,
　　　　the moon and the stars which thou hast established;
What is man that thou art mindful of him,
　　　　and the son of man that thou dost care for him?
Yet thou hast made him little less than God [the angels],
　　　　and dost crown him with glory and honor.
Thou hast given him dominion over the works of thy hands;
　　　　thou hast put all things under his feet . . .
　　　　　　　　　　　　　　　　　　　　—Psalm 8:3-6

Psalm 8 deals with two inseparably related questions: the question of who God is, and the question of who man is in God's creation. The psalm is closely related to the creation story in Genesis 1, a fact which is not surprising when one considers that both have their setting in the worship at the Jerusalem temple. The psalmist's affirmation that Yahweh has created man so that he falls short of the divine realm just "a little" is paralleled in the statement of Genesis 1 that God made man "in his image" and "according to his likeness." In both cases the intention is to say that man is made for *relationship* with God,[12] a relationship which elevates him above the natural world and enables him to have dominion over the realm of nature.

The concept of man's dominion over nature is revolutionary when measured against ancient religions which declared that the gods were natural powers and that man's life was embraced within the mysterious depth of nature, with its rhythmic cycles of fertility. The God of Israel is not a natural power: he transcends the realm of nature, for he is its Creator. And in a lesser sense man, though related to the animals, stands over against nature as the creature who is commissioned to have dominion over the works of God's creation, as one who is the representative or vicegerent of God's sovereignty (kingdom) on earth. This emptying nature of divinity has made possible a "scientific" approach to nature as a realm which man can study, explore, and use in the service of God. It is hardly accidental that the scientific movement, which has brought about revolutionary developments in the twentieth century on earth and in space, has been nourished in the soil of the Israelite-Christian tradition. The tremendous achievements of science in the fields of medicine, transportation, communication, and space exploration—to mention only a few—may be regarded as a partial fulfillment of the task which the Creator has given man in crowning him a king in his creation.

The other side of this picture, of course, is the somber consideration of the risk which God has taken in elevating man to this position of supremacy and honor. This risk is dramatically portrayed in the story of Paradise Lost (Gen. 2-3), which the editors of the Pentateuch included as a supplement to the creation story found at the beginning of the Bible. Man's position of lordship over the natural world may also tempt him to assert his independence from God and to use his God-given freedom in such a way that human history is converted into a scene of exploitation, warfare, and chaos. The biblical writers give us no simple assurance that man, who falls just short of the divine realm, will use his honored position to fulfill God's purpose in the natural realm and to order his historical life in accordance with God's will. This is the fundamental problem to which the Bible addresses itself: man's grandeur and his misery, his high calling and his lost opportunity. In our own time we can sense this problem clearly, as we see how the scientific exploits of man hold out the terrifying possibility of nuclear destruction or the carrying of man's military adventures into space. Moreover, we are painfully aware that man's scientific achievements may seriously upset the balance of nature, to the point where not only plant and animal life but human life itself may be threatened by the increasing pollution of air, earth, and water. The question for the future is whether man—as scientist, industrialist, technologist—can rise to the stature of manhood which he was given in the creation and can affirm with the psalmist of Israel that "the earth is the Lord's and the fullness thereof" (Ps. 24:1).

It should be clear from a consideration of the hymns listed in the above outline (p. 103), and especially those dealing with creation and history, that Israel's creation-faith is rooted primarily in an interpretation of man's history. The praise of the Creator does not result in a theoretical explanation of how the universe began, one which would compete with the hypotheses of modern science. The fundamental question is, rather, who God is (his Name), and who man is in the light of God's self-disclosure. The Creator whom Israel worships is the God who is "the first" and "the last" and who, like a musician, can grasp the melody of history in its totality, from the beginning to end.

Israel dares to confess that the purpose disclosed in her historical experience is the clue to the purpose which was initiated "in the beginning" and which will be brought to fulfillment "in the end." The self-disclosure of Yahweh to his people is the clue to understanding who we are, why we are here on earth, and where history is going. Hence the psalmist affirms that the word spoken to Israel is the word by which the heavens and the earth were created:

By the word of Yahweh the heavens were made,
      and all their host by the breath of his mouth.
He gathered the waters of the sea as in a bottle;
      he put the deeps in storehouses.

Let all the earth fear Yahweh,
      let all the inhabitants of the world stand in awe of
            him!
For he spoke, and it came to be;
      he commanded, and it stood forth.
                 —Psalm 33:6-9 (cf. Ps. 148:5-6)

In the same manner it is affirmed in the New Testament that God's word spoken in Jesus Christ is the disclosure of history's meaning, and hence the disclosure of the purpose underlying the whole creation. In him "everything" holds together meaningfully.

> *He is the image of the invisible God, the first-born of all creation; for in him all things were created, in heaven and on earth, visible and invisible, whether thrones or dominions or principalities or authorities —all things were created through him and for him. He is before all things, and in him all things hold together.*
>
>   —*Colossians 1:15-17*

HIS PRAISE FROM THE END OF THE EARTH

The emphasis in the Psalter upon the name of God raises a major question in our time. It would seem, at first glance, that the praise of Yahweh, the God known and worshiped in Israel, leads into a narrow religious understanding, a kind of theological isolationism. We live in a period when the cultures of East and West are coming into creative interrelationship—a development which has influenced our art and literature and to some extent our music. Symbolically, at least, two such different instruments as the violin and the Indian sitar have been brought together in concert, as when Yehudi Menuhin and Ravi Shankar performed a duet before the United Nations to commemorate the anniversary of the Declaration of Human Rights (December 10, 1967). In this day of expanding cultural and cosmic horizons many people are more interested in "duets" between, say, Christianity and Buddhism, than in returning to the solo performance of a theological particularism. Indeed, some hope that all the religious faiths of mankind will someday blend their witnesses in a symphony to the glory of "deity." How, then, does the emphasis on the Name make sense?

It should be said, in response to this question, that the psalmists' praise of Yahweh does not lead to a theological confinement within Israel's history but, rather, to a universalism which embraces all mankind and the whole cosmos. Israel's faith is rooted, as we have seen, in the human situation in which all men are involved. Man is a historical being, who remembers the past, lives toward the future, and is called to decide and act responsibly in the present. The questions, "Who am I? Where have I come from? Where am I going?" are not monopolized by a special people; they are inescapable human questions, raised by sensitive men who know that life is lived in the shadow of death and in the prospect of the ultimate dissolution of the earth (see Ps. 46:2). Israel's faith stands in opposition to any religion, ancient or modern, in which man "sees himself as real, i.e., as 'truly himself' only and precisely insofar as he ceases to be so"—only as (through the cultus) he flees from history into a timeless, changeless realm.[13] The Bible speaks to man who "thirsts for reality" and whose thirst can only be satisfied in history. It affirms that the God whose Name (identity) is disclosed in Israel's history is the God upon whom all men are dependent. The meaning of existence which Yahweh lays bare in Israel's historical experience is actually the meaning of the existence of every man. Thus the invocation to praise is addressed not just to Israel, but to all peoples and to "the ends of the earth":

> Sing to Yahweh a new song,
>> his praise from the end of the earth!
> Let the sea roar and all that fills it,
>> the coastlands and their inhabitants.
> Let the desert and its cities lift up their voice,
>> the villages that Kedar inhabits;
> let the inhabitants of Sela sing for joy,
>> let them shout from the top of the mountains.
> Let them give glory to Yahweh,
>> and declare his praise in the coastlands.
>> —Isaiah 42:10-12

Even the most remote and isolated places—Kedar (Jer. 49:28-29) and Sela (II Kings 14:7)—are embraced within the meaning of history which Yahweh discloses.

It is therefore significant that some of Israel's hymns move without a break from the praise of Yahweh the Creator to the praise of Yahweh as the Lord of history. We have already found this to be the case in a salvation history psalm like Psalm 136, which departs from the outline of Israel's old credo by prefixing to the sacred history the rehearsal of Yahweh's great deeds of creation (Ps. 136:4-9). This kind of praise finds even more magnificent expression in Psalm 33. Displaying the characteristic form of the hymn, it begins with an invocation to worship (vss. 1-3). Then with the motive-word "for" (*ki*) it moves into an exposition of the ground of praise.

> For the word of Yahweh is upright;
>> and all his work is done in faithfulness.
> He loves righteousness and justice;
>> the earth is full of the steadfast love of Yahweh.
>>> —Psalm 33:4-5

The psalmist expands this by saying, first, that it was by the word of Yahweh that the heavens and earth were made (vss. 6-9); and he continues by declaring that Yahweh's purpose rules the destinies of all the nations (vss. 10-19). The psalm concludes with an expression of trust in Yahweh, the Creator and Redeemer (vss. 20-22), thereby resounding the note struck at the beginning.

The spacious universalism of this psalm does not contradict the announcement that God has chosen to disclose his name within Israel's history. On the contrary, Yahweh's historical self-disclosure to Israel provides the basis for the universal horizons of thought. The revelation (word) of Yahweh is not only the inner meaning of the events of Israel's history; it is also the meaning of every individual's experience (see especially Pss. 103 and 113), the meaning of the history of mankind, and the meaning of the whole cosmos. This is not a far cry from the announcement made at the opening of the Gospel of John. Echoing the "in the beginning" of Genesis 1:1, this Gospel affirms that God's revelation in Christ was the Word by whom all things were created and in whom all things are sustained. And this word is not confined to a corner of history: it is "the true light that enlightens every man" (John 1:9).

6:

THINE

IS THE KINGDOM

With few exceptions the psalms considered in the previous chapters—the laments, thanksgivings, and hymns—may be called "cultic songs." These songs were designed for, or at least presupposed, a setting of worship in which the cultic community responded to the overtures of God toward his people in their ongoing history.[1] Of course, not *all* the Psalms were intended for use on cultic occasions in the temple. Some were intended for the circles of home or palace, some were to be sung by pilgrims on their journey or workers in the field, some were for teaching or private meditation and reflection. In many ways, however, the Psalms express the longing of the Israelite to "behold the face of God," that is, to be present at the temple where God reveals himself to the worshiping community.

As a hart longs
     for flowing streams,
so longs my soul
     for thee, O God.
My soul thirsts for God,
     for the living God.
When shall I come and behold
     the face of God?
         —Psalm 42:1-2

The Psalmist's consuming desire is to "dwell" (sojourn, visit) in the house of Yahweh (cf. 23:6), that is, to worship in the temple.

One thing have I asked of Yahweh,
　　that will I seek after;
that I may dwell in the house of Yahweh
　　all the days of my life,
to behold the beauty of Yahweh,
　　and to inquire in his temple.
　　　　　　　　　　—Psalm 27:4

The latter reference to seeing "the beauty of Yahweh" is particularly interesting. An Egyptian text speaks of "Ammon's beauty," and this has been plausibly interpreted to mean something very concrete: beholding the god's statue in the temple or in a ceremonial procession. However, since Israelite religion from the time of Moses prohibited statues (Ex. 20:4), this visual interpretation is excluded. It has been suggested that the phrase could refer to "seeing God's power and glory" (Ps. 63:2) in a cultic drama which symbolically represented God's appearance (theophany) to his people; or, of course, it could be merely a metaphorical expression for the nearness of God experienced in the temple services. In any case, the temple is the particular place where God's glory "dwells" (Ps. 26:8). Therefore a psalmist prays:

O send out thy light and thy truth;
　　let them lead me,
let them bring me to thy holy hill
　　and to thy dwelling!
Then I will go to the altar of God,
　　to God my exceeding joy;
And I will praise thee with the lyre,
　　O God, my God.
　　　　　　　　　　—Psalm 43:3-4

One of the most beautiful songs concerning the temple is Psalm 84, in which a psalmist envies the nesting birds that find security in the Jerusalem temple and exclaims that even one day spent in the temple courts is better than a thousand spent elsewhere.

The Psalms, then, lend no support to the notion that a person's relationship with God is his own private affair and that God is accessible outside the liturgical forms and sacraments of the worshiping community. On the contrary, the individual is related to God as a member of the covenant community. God, for his own part, can seek men in any way that he pleases; in his sovereign freedom he can display his justice and mercy to any man or people (see the story of Jonah). Yet if men would have access to God in worship, they must come to the place which he has chosen and seek him according to established cultic means. In the Psalter, therefore, the individual praises God in concert with the worshiping community:

O magnify Yahweh with me,
    and let us exalt his name together!
            —Psalm 34:3

LITURGIES OF THE TRIBAL FEDERATION

In the period before the formation of the state under David, when Israel was loosely bound together as a Tribal Confederacy, it was customary for people to gather from all the tribes of Israel to the central sanctuary, located first at Shechem (Josh. 24) and subsequently at Shiloh (I Sam. 1). The ancient covenant law specifically enjoined three annual pilgrimages: "Three times in the year shall all your males appear before Yahweh God, the God of Israel" (Ex. 23:14-17; 34:18, 22-23). These pilgrimage festivals, originally adopted from the Canaanite sacred calendar, coincided with the major agricultural seasons. The first, the Festival of Unleavened Bread (later associated with the Passover), was held in March-April at the time of the barley harvest; the second, the Festival of First Fruits (also called Weeks or Pentecost), occurred in May-June at the time of the wheat harvest; and the third, the Festival of Ingathering (also called Tabernacles), took place in September-October at the time of the grape and olive harvest.

Of these three festivals, the most important was the autumn vintage festival. This wine festival, held at the turn of the year according to the old agricultural calendar (and later connected with New Year's Day: *Rosh ha-Shana*), was celebrated with dancing and merrymaking (Judg. 21:19-23). It was a time of heavy drinking of new wine, to judge from Eli's suspicion that Hannah was "drunken" (I Sam. 1:14-15). However, what had originated as a Canaanite nature festival was radically transformed by being reinterpreted in terms of Israel's "salvation history." The custom—which has continued to the present day—of making huts or booths out of tree branches and erecting them in the vineyards while the grapes were being harvested, was reinterpreted as a commemoration of the time in the wilderness when Israel lived in huts or shelters (Lev. 23:43). (The Latin Vulgate translated the Hebrew word *sukkoth*, "huts" or "booths," as *tabernacula*, from which comes our word "tabernacles.")

Even in a very early period, before the time of David, the Israelites seem to have celebrated this festival as a time for renewing the covenant with Yahweh. In the service of worship the saving deeds of Yahweh in Israel's history were proclaimed, and the people were called upon to reaffirm their allegiance to the God of Israel. The structure of this covenant-renewal service has been reconstructed from Joshua 24 and related passages as follows:[2]

1. The call to assembly (Josh. 24:1)
2. Historical Prologue: a confessional summary of Yahweh's deeds of deliverance (Josh. 24:2-13)
3. Call to decision for or against Yahweh (Josh. 24:14-22)
4. Purification: removal of foreign gods (Josh. 24:23-24; cf. Gen. 35:1-4)
5. The renewal of the covenant (Josh. 24:25; cf. Ex. 24:4-8)
6. The reading of the covenant law (Josh. 24:25-26; cf. Ex. 24:7)
7. A ceremony of sanctions: the blessings and the curses (see Deut. 27:11-26; Josh. 8:30-35)
8. The dismissal of the congregation (Josh. 24:28)

Some of the elements of this covenant renewal service are present in contemporary worship services. It would be interesting to compare the form of this service with the Covenant Renewal Service of John Wesley, designed primarily for use at the turn of the year.[3]

This liturgical tradition persisted even after the unity of the Davidic kingdom was broken and the people were politically divided into North Israel (Ephraim) and South Israel (Judah). According to I Kings 12:32-33, Jeroboam I (922-901 B.C.), the first king of North Israel, instituted an autumn festival "like the feast that was in Judah"—a reference to the harvest or New Year Festival (Tabernacles) which was celebrated in the south. For political reasons he wanted to deter his people from making pilgrimages to the temple of Jerusalem, and so he revived the old covenant renewal festival that had been celebrated during the days of the Tribal Confederacy (the time of the Judges). Subsequently, Bethel became one of the major cultic centers in the north, a fact recognized by the prophet Amos more than a century later when he traveled from his home in the south to Bethel, where "a temple of the kingdom" was located (Amos 7:13). Amos' contemporary, Hosea, seems to have referred to the Fall festival in the north (Hos. 9:5, "the day of the feast of Yahweh"). Undoubtedly some of the psalms now found in the Psalter were used in the Bethel cult. It may be surmised that, after the fall of the northern kingdom under Assyrian aggression in 722 B.C., these psalms were taken over in southern Israel (Judah) where they were adapted for use in the festivals of Zion.

It is difficult to ascertain which psalms actually belonged to the covenant renewal festival celebrated in the northern kingdom.[4] Two psalms, however, clearly seem to be liturgies for that occasion.

COVENANT RENEWAL LITURGIES

50 "Our God comes, he does not keep silence"
*81 "Hear, O my people, while I admonish you!"

Notice that Psalm 81 closely parallels the liturgy of covenant renewal found in Joshua 24. It begins with an invocation to praise "the God of Jacob" at the sanctuary "on our feast day," presumably a reference to the Fall festival (vss. 1-5a). Then comes a reminder, perhaps given by a cultic priest or prophet, of what Yahweh has done for his people, beginning with the deliverance from Egyptian bondage (vss. 5b-10). The psalm reaches a climax with an appeal to the people to repent and reaffirm their loyalty to Yahweh, and to "walk in [his] ways" (vss. 11-16), that is, to accept anew the duties of the covenant law. The theological assumption of Psalm 81 is that of the Mosaic covenant: "*If* you will obey my voice and keep my covenant, you shall be my own possession among all peoples" (Ex. 19:5). This conditional covenant carries consequences which prophets like Hosea spelled out clearly: disobedience results in divine judgment and the dissolution of the covenant relationship—"You are not my people and I am not your God" (Hos. 1:8b). According to this Mosaic covenant theology, the sufferings and evils of history are traced to a fault in man's will. Those who "sow the wind" shall "reap the whirlwind" (Hos. 8:7) in the historical arena.

THE FESTIVAL OF ZION

Psalms like these may go back to a liturgical tradition of the Tribal Confederacy that was kept alive in North Israel. The Psalter in its present form, however, has been shaped in the circles of South Israel (Judah) and represents the liturgical usage of the Jerusalem temple. This is evident from the numerous references to Zion, the old name for the pre-Israelite fortified hill. Even more significant, however, are numerous passages in the Psalter which reflect the theological outlook of the Davidic court. The rise of David as king and the selection of Jerusalem as the place of the central sanctuary had a far-reaching influence upon Israel's worship, and specifically upon the covenant festival celebrated in the Jerusalem temple. Jerusalem theologians wanted to say that the rule of David was the fulfillment of the sacred history which began with the migration of Abraham from Mesopotamia (Gen. 12:1-9). Furthermore, they declared that, in raising up David to be king and in choosing Zion as His dwelling place, Yahweh had led Israel into a new era which required a new theological understanding. This is the theme of Psalm 78.

To understand this new kind of covenant theology which centered in David and Zion it is necessary to turn to the portion of the David story found in two important chapters: II Samuel 6 and 7. The first of these chapters relates that David, desiring to unify his kingdom on the basis of the religious loyalty of the Tribal Confederacy, brought the Ark of the Covenant—the portable "throne" on which Yahweh was invisibly enthroned in the midst of his people during their wars and wanderings—into his new capital of Jerusalem with the intention of housing it in a temple. Jerusalem was not to be just the city of David but "Zion, city of our God," the locus of Yahweh's real presence in the midst of his people. The last part of Psalm 24 is an ancient liturgy, possibly as old as the time of Solomon, which undoubtedly was used in reenacting the processional bearing of the Ark into the Jerusalem temple where Yahweh was acclaimed as King. As the procession reaches the gates of Zion, voices sing antiphonally:

Lift up your heads, O gates!
    and be lifted up, O ancient doors!
    that the King of glory may come in!

Who is the King of glory?
    Yahweh, strong and mighty,
    Yahweh mighty in battle!
                —Psalm 24:7-8

In the following verses the ritual is repeated and once again Yahweh, enthroned invisibly on the Ark, is acclaimed as the glorious King.

Returning for a moment to the story in II Samuel 6 and 7, David wanted to build Yahweh a "house" (temple), com rable in magnificence to his own palace. The prophet Nathan, however, opposed this plan and delivered to the king an oracle in which Yahweh promised David to build *him* a "house" (dynasty) which would stand in perpetuity.

" 'Yahweh declares to you that Yahweh will make you a house. When your days are fulfilled and you lie down with your fathers, I will raise up your son after you, who shall come forth from your body, and I will establish his kingdom. He shall build a house for my name, and I will establish the throne of his kingdom for ever. I will be his father, and he shall be my son. When he commits iniquity, I will chasten him with the rod of men, with the stripes of the sons of men; but I will not take my steadfast love [ḥesed] from him, as I took it from Saul, whom I put away from before you. And your house and your kingdom shall be made sure for ever before me; your throne shall be established for ever.' "

—II Samuel 7:11b-16

Notice that this covenant, unlike the Mosaic covenant, is not couched in the conditional terms: "If you will obey my voice . . . you shall be my people"; rather, the Davidic covenant is fundamentally unconditional. God's relationship with his people, mediated through the reigning Davidic king, the "Anointed One" (Hebrew: "messiah"), is based solely on his ḥesed ("steadfast love," RSV) or covenant promise of loyalty to David. This Davidic covenant theology provides the theological background for the New Testament proclamation that God's relationship with his people, mediated through Jesus, his Anointed (Greek: "Christ"), is grounded unconditionally in his grace, and is not contingent upon the human fulfillment of conditions.

The Fall festival in Jerusalem, then, acquired a special character owing to the celebration of the simultaneous founding of the Jerusalem sanctuary and the Davidic dynasty. According to this covenant theology, Yahweh is *the King* par excellence, as Isaiah perceived in his inaugural vision.

I saw Yahweh sitting upon a throne, high and lifted up; and his train filled the temple.

—Isaiah 6:1

The King, whose throne is in heaven (Ps. 11:4), has chosen Zion as the center of his presence in the midst of his people; and he has chosen the Davidic king as the representative of his rule on earth.

Several psalms express this theological understanding of God's relation to his people:

Psalm 78* *A recitation of Yahweh's great deeds*

> This psalm (see chap. 2) contains a long summary of Yahweh's historical deeds, beginning with the Exodus (vss. 1-66). It is particularly interesting because the psalmist affirms that the old sacred history has come to an end, owing to the unfaithfulness of North Israel ("the tent of Joseph"). Yahweh has made a new beginning in history by raising up David to be king and by selecting Zion as his special abode (vss. 67-72).

Psalm 132* *A liturgy commemorating Yahweh's covenant with David and his choice of Zion*

> Here the story in II Samuel 7 is clearly in mind. The psalmist begins by recalling David's intention to build a sanctuary for Yahweh (vss. 1-5). He continues with a ritual which was undoubtedly used during the processional bearing of the Ark into the Jerusalem temple (vss. 6-10). Recalling the ancient Song of the Ark (Num. 10:35-36), the worshipers affirm that Yahweh has already found a dwelling-place:

Arise, O Yahweh, and go to thy resting place,
    thou and the ark of thy might.
Let thy priests be clothed with righteousness,
    and let thy saints shout for joy.
                        —Psalm 132:8-9

The psalm concludes (vss. 11-18) with a reaffirmation of Yahweh's covenant with David and his choice of Zion as the center of his earthly presence.

Psalm 89 *A hymn and a lament based on Yahweh's covenant with David*

The first part of this psalm (vss. 1-37) is a hymn which praises Yahweh for the "steadfast love" which he manifested in his covenant with David. The hymn echoes the covenant theology of II Samuel 7 and, in addition, strikes the note that Yahweh's power as Creator upholds the stability and continuity of the Davidic throne. The second part of the psalm is a lament (vss. 38-51) in which the psalmist complains that God apparently has forsaken the covenant with David, as evidenced by the defeat of the king in battle. He appeals to Yahweh to remove the calamity and thus to reaffirm the covenant loyalty which he once swore to David.

THE LORD'S ANOINTED

This Davidic covenant theology, with its twofold emphasis upon the choosing of David and the choosing of Zion, casts light on two groups of psalms in the Psalter. The first group consists of those psalms in which the king is the central figure.

   *2 "You are my son, today I have begotten you"
       (Coronation)

  *18 "With the loyal thou dost show thyself loyal"
       (Thanksgiving for victory)

  20 "Give victory to the king, O Yahweh"
       (Prayer for the king's victory)

  21 "In thy strength the king rejoices" (Coronation)

  45 "Your divine throne endures for ever"
       (Royal wedding)

  72 "Give the king thy justice, O God"
       (Coronation)

 101 "I will sing of loyalty and of justice"
       (Coronation oath)

*110 "A priest for ever after the order of
       Melchizedek" (Coronation)

 144 (1-11) "Rescue me from the many waters"
       (Royal lament)

Israel lived in an environment in which the king's authority was based upon a mythology that made him the representative and upholder of the divine order. An ancient Sumerian king list, for instance, traces kingship to a divine origin in primeval time, "when kingship was lowered from heaven." [5] Some of this "court poetry" was adopted in Israel, as can be seen from the psalms listed above. For instance, Psalm 45, the royal wedding psalm (probably a psalm from North Israel), speaks of the king in such extravagant language that it sounds as if he is being deified. The address to the king in verse 6 could be translated "your throne, O God" (RSV margin), although the *Revised Standard Version* glosses over the problem by translating "your divine throne." More significant than this enigmatic text is the aspect of Davidic theology which establishes a special relationship between Yahweh and the Davidic king: "I will be his father, and he shall be my son" (II Sam. 7:14; cf. Ps. 89:26-27).

Israel, however, did not adopt the mythical view of the king without modification. According to Israelite tradition, kingship emerged out of the harsh realities of secular politics, particularly the crisis caused by the Philistine attempt to build an empire in Palestine. Above all, the institution of kingship in Israel was connected with Israel's sacred history, that is, the formation of Israel as the People of God. The raising up of David was a decisive act of Yahweh in Israel's history.[6] Therefore, the royal psalms, despite their dependence upon court poetry, do not confer divinity upon the king. The king is God's "son" by adoption, as we read clearly in Psalm 2:7 (quoted in Acts 13:33), that is, he is *chosen* to perform a particular role in the history of God with his people Israel. The king's authority is not absolute: it is derived from Yahweh who is *the* King. Consequently the king rules as Yahweh's representative who obtains justice for the weak and the oppressed (Ps. 72).

The portrait presented in these royal psalms does not conform to any specific king of the house of David. Rather, it depicts the *type* of the true king who perfectly combines power and goodness. Since the type was not perfectly embodied in any of the Davidic kings it is understandable that, in the course of time, especially after the collapse of the Davidic monarchy in 587 B.C., these psalms were interpreted to refer to the "Anointed One" (Messiah) of the future, who would come in God's good time to rule over his Kingdom. Thus in the New Testament the opening words of Psalm 110— where the Lord (the God of Israel) addresses "my lord" (the Davidic king about to ascend the throne)—are taken to refer to the Messiah (Matt. 22:44; Acts 2:34; I Cor. 15:25; Eph. 1:20; Heb. 1:3, 13).

Also related to the Davidic covenant theology is the group of psalms designated as "songs of Zion"—a title derived from Psalm 137:3. These psalms express the view that Yahweh has chosen Zion as the earthly center of his presence in the midst of his people; accordingly, if men would have access to him in worship, they must come to "the place" (sanctuary) which he has chosen.

SONGS OF ZION

*46 "Yahweh of hosts is with us"
48 "His holy mountain . . . is the joy of all the earth"
76 "Surely the wrath of men shall praise thee"
*84 "How lovely is thy dwelling place, O Yahweh of hosts!"
87 "Glorious things are spoken of you, O city of God"
*122 "Pray for the peace of Jerusalem!"

One of these psalms, Psalm 46, provided the keynote of Luther's great hymn of the Reformation: "A Mighty Fortress Is Our God." In the first strophe of this psalm (vss. 1-3) the psalmist confesses that man's security is in God alone who sustains the meaning of life, even though the earth should be engulfed in the waters of chaos. In the second strophe (vss. 4-7) he affirms that Jerusalem, the City of God, will remain secure for it is the center of God's presence on earth. In the final strophe (vss. 8-11) he announces that in the time when God's sovereignty over all the nations is acknowledged, wars will cease to the ends of the earth. Above the tumult and shouting of history is heard the command of the God who is Creator and Lord: "Be still and know [Moffatt: "give in, and admit"] that I am God." Originally each of these three strophes was probably punctuated with the choral refrain: "Yahweh of hosts is with us; the God of Jacob is our refuge."

In our age of universalism this emphasis upon the centrality of Zion has a strange ring. Today people suppose that if God reveals himself at all, he could reveal himself in one place as well as in another. Why, then, should Zion be acclaimed as "the joy of all the earth," as the Center ("navel") "where heaven and earth meet," [7] as the holy mountain from which erupts a life-giving stream to renew the wilderness? (Ps. 46:4; Ezek. 47:1-12; cf. Rev. 22:1-2) The answer is that these psalms, like the Bible as a whole, express a universalism which arises out of historical particularism. To the psalmists, Zion was the center of historical meaning which God had disclosed to Israel and, *through* Israel, to the whole world. The meaning unveiled in Israel's history is not confined to Israel; it is the meaning of all human existence with its history of wars, animosities, and misunderstandings—the history portrayed in the story of the Tower of Babel (Gen. 11:1-9). In a passage about the "last days"—the consummation of history— it is announced that ultimately all men will make a pilgrimage to Zion. Then they shall say to one another:

> "Come, let us go up to the mountain of Yahweh,
>> to the house of the God of Jacob;
> that he may teach us his ways,
>> and that we may walk in his paths."
> For out of Zion shall go forth the law,
>> and the word of Yahweh from Jerusalem.
> He shall judge between the nations,
>> and shall decide for many peoples;
> and they shall beat their swords into plowshares,
>> and their spears into pruning hooks;

> *nation shall not lift up sword against nation,*
> > *neither shall they learn war any more.*
> > > —*Isaiah 2:3-4; cf. Micah 4:1-3*

The Christian faith, with its spacious universalism, does not surrender the centrality of Zion. The whole drama of God's dealings with his people leads up to the appearance of the Messiah in Jerusalem, and to his death and victory there—the crucial event which is reenacted in Christian worship. Zion is the historical center around which God has gathered his people, the membership of which is determined by God's choosing, not by man's standards. It is theologically appropriate, then, that Psalm 87:3 became the text of Augustine's monumental work *The City of God.* Centuries later, the same text inspired the composition of the hymn by John Newton (1725-1807), "Glorious Things of Thee Are Spoken, Zion, City of Our God."

THE KINGDOM OF GOD

In the Jerusalem cult the themes of the choosing of David and the choosing of Zion were based upon the primary theme of the kingship of Yahweh over Israel, the nations, and the cosmos. We turn then, in conclusion, to a number of "enthronement psalms" which deal specifically with this motif. In the prophecy of Second Isaiah, the theme of these psalms was transposed into the key of the "good news" that was later heard in Jesus' preaching (Mark 1:15).

> *How beautiful upon the mountains*
> > *are the feet of him who brings good tidings,*
> *who publishes peace, who brings good tidings of good,*
> > *who publishes salvation,*
> > > *who says to Zion, "Your God reigns."*
> > > > —*Isaiah 52:7*

All the psalms falling under this category are hymns. A prominent feature is the cultic exclamation *Yahweh malak*, "Yahweh is king" ("The Lord reigns," RSV).

ENTHRONEMENT PSALMS

29 "Yahweh sits enthroned as king for ever"
*47 "God is the king of all the earth"
93 "Thy throne is established from of old"
*95 "Yahweh is a great King above all gods"
*96 "Say among the nations, 'Yahweh reigns!'"
97 "Yahweh reigns; let the earth rejoice"
*98 "O sing to Yahweh a new song"
*99 "Yahweh reigns; let the peoples tremble!"
(See also Psalm 24, an entrance liturgy.)

These hymns presuppose the centrality of Zion, where Yahweh is magnified in the praises of his people (e.g., Pss. 96:6; 97:8; 99:2, 9). It is clear, however, that Yahweh's rule is not confined to Zion. The whole earth—and indeed the entire cosmos—is full of his glory. In these psalms the "salvation history" is noticeably sublimated, if not forgotten, except for a few pale allusions (e.g., 99:6-8). Here the God of Israel is extolled as the king of the nations and of the universe. Indeed, the peoples of the earth—represented by their princes—have become members of the People of God.

God reigns over the nations;
    God sits on his holy throne.
The princes of the peoples gather
    as the people of the God of Abraham.
For the shields [rulers] of the earth belong to God;
    he is highly exalted!
                                                —Psalm 47:8-9

The label "enthronement psalms" is a concession to the view, which has been widely accepted during the past generation of biblical scholarship, that at the turn of the year worshipers came to the Jerusalem temple to celebrate Yahweh's accession to his throne and the re-establishment of his kingship over all powers hostile to his rule. The Scandinavian scholar, Sigmund Mowinckel, has argued with considerable persuasiveness that the Fall festival celebrated in Jerusalem was patterned after festivals of divine kingship known among Israel's neighbors.[8] The chief example is the Babylonian New Year's festival, the *akitu*, at which the Babylonian creation myth was recited and reenacted. The myth depicts the violent struggle between the young god Marduk, and the goddess Tiamat, the dragon of chaos, and her chaotic allies. Victorious in the conflict, the divine warrior was acclaimed king in the council of the gods and the hymnic cry was raised: "Marduk has become king." The myth portrays man's involvement in the processes of nature which, moving in a circle, ever return to the beginning when the god must win a new victory over the powers of darkness and chaos.

Since Israel's worship was profoundly influenced by the surrounding culture, it is tempting to interpret these "enthronement" psalms in the light of cultic practice in Mesopotamia and Canaan. Some scholars argue that the cultic exclamation *Yahweh malak* should be translated, "Yahweh has become king," in which case the Jerusalem cult would have celebrated Yahweh's accession to his throne as king. To be sure, Hebrew grammar permits this translation. But it is exceedingly doubtful whether the Israelite faith, even in the cosmopolitan atmosphere of Jerusalem, adopted wholesale the pagan view that man's existence is caught up in the cycle of nature which ever returns to its beginning, at which time there is a new creation and God ascends his throne once again. These psalms are explicit in saying that Yahweh's throne is established "from of old," his kingdom is "from everlasting" (Ps. 93:2). His kingship is not contingent upon winning a new victory at the turn of the year. The God who established his kingdom of old, and who will come in power to establish his kingdom with finality, is *now* enthroned upon the praises of his people. Past, present, and future are united in the cultic exclamation, "Yahweh is King!"

These psalms show how Israel appropriated the mythical imagery of the ancient world and converted it to the praise of Yahweh, the King of the Universe. Worship at Jerusalem was profoundly infused with faith in Yahweh as Creator. In North Israel, as we have seen, there was a greater stress upon the conditional Mosaic covenant and, consequently, the threat of social disaster, owing to the persistent and defiant exercise of man's freedom. In the south (Judah), however, there was more concern for the order and stability represented by the Davidic dynasty. The interpreters who developed the royal covenant theology wanted to say that the order represented by the Davidic dynasty was not just a political achievement: it was somehow related to the purpose of God who, at the time of creation, established the earth on firm foundations and brought order out of chaos. When a Davidic king (Uzziah) died and society was threatened with confusion, Isaiah envisioned *the* King, seated upon his heavenly throne, high and lifted up (Isa. 6:1, 5).

In these psalms the ancient myth of the creator's victory over the powers of chaos (the "floods," the "sea," the Deep) is used poetically to express the faith that no powers—whether historical enemies, death, or anything else in creation—can subvert God's rule. He is enthroned triumphantly over the powers which threaten to plunge history into meaningless disorder and chaos.

The floods have lifted up, O Yahweh,
      the floods have lifted up their voice,
      the floods lift up their roaring.
Mightier than the thunders of many waters,
      mightier than the waves of the sea,
      Yahweh on high is mighty!
                    —Psalm 93:3-4

In this faith the writer of the 46th Psalm can say that even though the earth should be shaken with cosmic tumult and the waters of chaos threaten to overwhelm, God still remains the source of history's meaning and the unchallengeable sovereign over the nations. His everlasting covenant stands.

Therefore we will not fear though the earth should change,
      though the mountains shake in the heart of the sea;
though its waters roar and foam,
      though the mountains tremble with its tumult.
                    —Psalm 46:2-3

While stressing Yahweh's everlasting kingship from the very beginning, these psalms also look toward the future when his kingdom will be finally realized. The worshiping community, of course, rejoiced in the present tokens of Yahweh's kingship, which perhaps were re-enacted or contemporized in worship.

Come and see what God has done:
      he is terrible in his deeds among men.
                    —Psalm 66:5

Yet even for those who *see* in faith, the sovereignty of God is not beyond the shadow of doubt. Men still have to wrestle with the dark enigma of evil which cannot be traced exclusively to a fault in man's will. They must still live in a world where the weak are oppressed by the mighty, where wrongs are perpetrated in the name of God, and where death imposes the final threat to the goodness of the life which God has ordained. An important dimension of these psalms, then, is their "eschatological outlook." In hymnic tones they express the expectation that the King is coming on the stage of history to "judge" the earth, to establish his kingdom.

Let the sea roar, and all that fills it;
     the world and those who dwell in it!
Let the floods clap their hands;
     let the hills sing for joy together
before Yahweh, for he comes
     to judge the earth.
He will judge the world with righteousness,
     and the people with equity.
          —Psalm 98:7-9; cf. 96:10-13

Here the verb "judge" means much more than our English word suggests. It refers to the King's exercise of wisdom and power which overcomes injustice and vindicates the oppressed. God's judgment is the expression of his saving power.

Today the exclamation "The Lord is King" is raised hymnically in services of Christian worship. Indeed, in some Christian circles a new feast is being celebrated in the autumn known as "The Feast of Christ the King." The Christian church reads the enthronement psalms in the context of the gospel that, through Jesus Christ, God has inaugurated his kingdom by striking the decisive blow against all powers of oppression, darkness, chaos, and death. Those who celebrate Christ's kingship in the festivals of his enthronement are summoned to new action and responsibility in the world, whatever the odds may be, knowing that the decisive victory has already been won. Yet the church also lives toward the final establishment of God's kingdom when his purpose will be completely realized, when man will become fully human in a new creation—"a new heaven and a new earth." In the time between the advent of the King and the final establishment of the Kingdom, Christians also pray the enthronement psalms in the spirit of the Lord's Prayer:

> *"Thy kingdom come.*
> *Thy will be done.*
> > *On earth as it is in heaven."*
> > > *—Matthew 6:10*

7:

A TABLE

PREPARED

In the sixteenth century Joseph ben Ephraim Qaro (1488-1575), a persecuted Spanish Jew who migrated to Palestine, produced a monumental summary of Jewish law under the title *Shulhan Aruk* (Table Prepared). The title, which Qaro took from the well-known passage in the Twenty-third Psalm, was by no means inappropriate for a work designed to instruct in the Law. This is clear when one understands that the Psalter, in its final form, was not just a hymnbook intended for use in the temple of Jerusalem. The editors of this collection also had in mind the use of the Psalms for religious education and spiritual sustenance—as is evident from the position at the beginning of the Psalter of two psalms, one dealing with the study of the Law and the other with the Messiah (Pss. 1 and 2). With these psalms the editors invited their readers "to choose the right path to the Messianic glory: the study of the law and the obedience toward the word of God." [1]

The final adaptation of the Psalter for use in instruction as well as in worship took place during the period following the return from Babylonian exile in the sixth century B.C. At this time a new form of gathering—possibly related to the situation of worship in exile—gained importance in the Israelite community and eventually developed into the assembly known as the synagogue. Even after the temple at Jerusalem was rebuilt, the people found that more and more their life centered in the kind of gathering which provided occasions for prayer and edification. In this new community setting many psalms became detached from their original cultic situations in temple worship and were read simply as "spiritual songs"—affirmations of trust, expressions of delight in the Law, and "wisdom" meditations upon the problems of existence. The new style of synagogue worship had a profound influence upon the early Christian community which was also concerned with "the right path to the Messianic glory."

SPIRITUAL SONGS

Previously we have noticed that the type of psalm called a lament moves quickly from a cry out of distress toward an expression of trust in God. Frequently this note of confidence is introduced by a conjunction (in Hebrew) which is translated by an adversative: "but," "yet," "nevertheless." *In spite of* his affliction the psalmist affirms his faith in Yahweh. For example:[2]

> But I trust in thee, O Yahweh,
> I say, "Thou art my God."
> My times are in thy hand . . .
> —Psalm 31:14-15*a*

There are a number of psalms, however, in which the motif of trust is developed as a self-contained song. These "songs of trust" have been plausibly explained as an independent development of the confession of trust which is a characteristic feature of the lament. They provide evidence of the way in which an important element of a psalm could become detached from a cultic form and setting and, with a freedom of its own, come to be a "spiritual song."

11 "In Yahweh I take refuge"

16 "In thy presence there is fulness of joy"

*23 "Yahweh is my shepherd, I shall not want"

*27 (1-6) "Yahweh is my light and my salvation"
(The second part of the psalm is a lament.)

62 "For God alone my soul waits in silence"

*63 "Thy steadfast love is better than life"

*91 "He will give his angels charge of you"

*121 "My help comes from Yahweh, who made heaven and earth"

125 "Those who trust in Yahweh are like Mount Zion"

131 "Like a child that is quieted is my soul"

(Psalm 4 is sometimes classified as a song of trust rather than an individual lament. In this list Psalm 63 may be regarded as an individual lament, and Psalm 125 may be considered a group lament. The line between the two types—the lament and the song of trust —often cannot be drawn sharply.)

In these psalms of trust we find various references to cultic actions such as the offering of sacrifices (Ps. 4:5), singing and dancing before Yahweh, or sojourning (dwelling) in Yahweh's "tent" (Ps. 27:4-6). The question may be raised, however, as to whether this traditional language, which was originally associated with worship services, came to be "spiritually interpreted" (Eissfeldt), that is, whether the language is now metaphorical. Certainly the primary concern of the psalmists is the sense of the nearness and saving power of God, which the people once experienced in the temple cult. In a later period, when the temple cult had lost its centrality for many people, "the concrete experience of the nearness of God in the Temple," as Artur Weiser observes, was "expanded and deepened" and thus the old language was interpreted symbolically.[3] This emancipation of the language of the psalms from the sphere of worship in the Jerusalem temple took place, as we have already noted, during the postexilic period when the synagogue began to occupy an important place in the life of the people. And this development, in turn, paved the way for the time when men were to hear that God is not to be worshiped exclusively in any geographical sphere, whether in Shechem (as the Samaritans advocated) or in Jerusalem (as the Jews claimed); rather, "the true worshipers will worship the Father in spirit and truth" (John 4:23-24).

THE SHEPHERD'S PSALM

As an illustration of the songs of trust, we turn to the well-known Twenty-third Psalm. By virtue of its profound simplicity and matchless beauty this psalm has touched the hearts of countless people down through the centuries. Here is a poem which children have learned by heart, which has sustained the mature in the perplexities of life, and which has been a peaceful benediction on the lips of the dying. No single psalm has expressed more powerfully man's prayer of confidence "out of the depths" to the God whose purpose alone gives meaning to the span of life, from womb to tomb. Since the Twenty-third Psalm is so familiar, it may be well to read it in a fresh translation:

Yahweh is my Shepherd, nothing do I lack.
> In grassy meadows he makes me repose,
> By quiet waters he leads me.
> He revives my whole being!
> He guides me into the right paths, for the honor of
> > his Name.

Even when I go through the valley of deep darkness,
    I fear nothing sinister;
    for You are at my side!
    Your rod and staff reassure me.

You spread out before me a table,
    in sight of those who threaten me.
    You pour upon my head festive oil.
    My cup is brimming over!

Certainly, divine goodness and grace attend me throughout
    all my days,
    and I shall be a guest in Yahweh's house as long
    as I live.[4]

                            —Psalm 23

The major problem in interpreting this psalm is that it presents two images which seem to be inconsistent. In verses 1-4 Yahweh is portrayed as the Good Shepherd who cares for his flock; in verses 5 and 6, on the other hand, Yahweh is the Host who offers hospitality to a guest and protects him from enemies. In German it can be said, with a euphonious play on words, that Yahweh is *mein Hirt und mein Wirt* (my shepherd and my host), but in the poem itself the images do not seem to harmonize so nicely. What do the shepherd and the host really have to do with one another?

This problem begins to resolve itself when we project ourselves imaginatively out of our industrial milieu into the pastoral way of life which still prevails in some parts of the world today. The shepherd can be portrayed from two standpoints. He is the protector of the sheep as they wander in search of grazing land. Yet he is also the protector of the traveler who finds hospitality in his tent from the dangers and enemies of the desert.[5] Even today the visitor to certain parts of the Middle East can see the scene which lies at the basis of the psalm: the black camel's hair tent where the traveler receives Bedouin hospitality, and the surrounding pastureland where the sheep graze under the protection of the shepherd. In Psalm 23 Yahweh is portrayed as the Shepherd in both aspects of the shepherd's life: as the Leader of the flock, and as the hospitable Host.

In the first part of the psalm, the psalmist likens his trust in Yahweh to that of sheep who confidently follow the shepherd as he leads them to green pastures and by quiet waters. This image is found repeatedly in the Old Testament (Pss. 80:1; 95:7; 100:3; Isa. 40:11; 49:9f.; 63:14; Ezekiel 34:10ff.). It is recapitulated in the New Testament in the parable of the lost sheep (Luke 15:3-7) and in the Johannine picture of Jesus Christ as the Good Shepherd (John 10:1-18). The image is admirably suited to express the understanding that man is not the ultimate measure of things, the controller of his world, or the determiner of his destiny. Yahweh, the psalmist affirms, is Israel's Maker; therefore the people belong to him and depend upon him, as sheep are related to their shepherd (see Pss. 95:6-7; 100:3). Of course, the image of the shepherd and his flock should not be understood merely in an idyllic sense. In the ancient Near East the king was regarded as the shepherd of his people. To address Yahweh as Shepherd was to acknowledge him as King (cf. Isa. 40:11).

This confidence that Yahweh is Israel's shepherd, which the psalmist personally appropriates by saying: "my shepherd," leads immediately to the affirmation that nothing more is needful—a statement which sounds somewhat strange in a commercialized world where the media of communication conspire to prove how much we are lacking. The psalmist's thought is echoed in many other psalms; for example:

Whom have I in heaven but thee?
>and there is nothing upon earth that I desire
>>besides thee.
My flesh and my heart may fail,
>but God is the strength of my heart
>>and my portion for ever.
>>>—Psalm 73:25-26

The psalmist does not espouse here an anemic faith
which turns away from the experiences of this life and
seeks fulfillment in some higher realm. On the contrary,
he testifies that his faith in God has repeatedly renewed
his life at the very core of his being (the Hebrew *nefesh*,
translated "soul" by the RSV at vs. 3*a*, really means
"my self," "my being"). He discerns a meaning flowing
through his life, which he can account for only by saying that Yahweh, like a shepherd who guides his sheep
into the right trails (the trails which are beneficial for
the flock), has been directing his life along a course
which leads toward fulfillment. The psalmist is aware
of the threats to his existence (cf. Ps. 5:8); but
even more he is aware of God's saving action bestowed
only for the sake of his divine honor, that is, because
God's nature (Name) is gracious. (See the discussion
of God's Name, chap. 5.) Just as the sheep do not always
pasture in verdant meadows or drink at quiet waters but
at times must walk precariously through the dark and
narrow valley where wild beasts and other dangers
lurk, so the psalmist affirms that God has guided him
through experiences which put him under trial or
brought him to the point of death. The familiar translation "the shadow of death" goes beyond the meaning
of the Hebrew term which means "deep darkness"
(Amos 5:8; Isa. 9:2; Ps. 44:19). Yet this secondary interpretation is consistent with the original meaning, for
in the view of the psalmists the power of death en-

croaches into a person's life when the vitality of his life is weakened. (See the discussion of death in chap. 4.)

In the second part of the psalm (vss. 5-6) the imagery shifts to the shepherd as host. According to the Bedouin law of hospitality, once a traveler is received into the shepherd's tent, and especially once his host has spread food before him, he is guaranteed immunity from enemies who may be attempting to overtake him. In pastoral circles no human protection is greater than that afforded by the hospitality of a Bedouin chief. So the psalmist expresses his trust in the Good Shepherd by saying that in Yahweh's tent he finds a protecting and gracious welcome. This divine hospitality is not just a temporary reprieve but a limitless protection from the powers that threaten his existence. The Host's tent is none other than the temple, as in Psalm 27:1-6 which closely parallels the thought of Psalm 23.

For he will hide me in his shelter
    in the day of trouble;
he will conceal me under the cover of his tent,
    he will set me high upon a rock.
                  —Psalm 27:5, cf. 61:4

The psalmist declares that in Yahweh's house ("tent") a table is prepared before him (perhaps a reference to a sacrificial meal in the temple; Ps. 22:26) and he is given the most cordial welcome—right in sight of his enemies. (See Ps. 27:6, and the discussion of the enemies, chap. 3.) Now it is no longer his enemies who "pursue" him; rather, it is Yahweh's grace and goodness that follow after him as long as he lives.

Some commentators have suggested that the Shepherd's Psalm was composed by a person who in the maturity of life looked back across the years and traced the purpose of God throughout his lifetime. One commentator writes:

> The sentiments of an almost childlike trust which the poet is able to express in this psalm are, however, by no means the product of a carefree unconcern characteristic of young people; on the contrary, they are the mature fruit of a heart which, having passed through many bitter experiences and having fought many battles (vss. 4, 5), had been allowed to find at the decline of life in its intimate communion with God (vss. 2, 6) the serenity of a contented spirit— peace of mind (vs. 6) and, in all dangers, strength.[6]

Perhaps it is fair to deduce this much from the psalm. In any case, the language has spoken to many people with increasing depth of meaning through the maturing years which hasten toward the "deep darkness." And when the psalm is read from the standpoint of Christian faith, it speaks of a table graciously spread, not only in the presence of the hostile powers of this age but also in the presence of "the last enemy" (I Cor. 15:26).

MEDITATIONS ON THE GOOD LIFE

In the Psalter we find a number of psalms which reflect the wisdom movement. This movement, as we know increasingly from archaeology and the study of ancient culture, was diffused throughout the whole ancient Near East—Egypt, Canaan, the fringes of Arabia, Asia Minor, Mesopotamia. Very early this movement made its impact on Israel, with the result that Solomon came to be regarded as the patron of wisdom, and important wisdom writings, such as Proverbs and Ecclesiastes, were attributed to him. In Israel, however, the wisdom movement, though having no essential relation to Yahweh's historical actions with his people Israel ("salvation history"), developed a distinctive Israelite accent, as evidenced in the proverb: "The fear of Yahweh is the beginning of wisdom" (Prov. 9:10; Job 28:28; Ps. 111:10). Israel's sages insisted that wisdom does not come just from observing human conduct or through rational reflection on the teachings handed down in the wisdom schools. Rather, the "beginning" (that is, the foundation or the core) of wisdom is *faith* —faith in Yahweh, the God who is known and worshiped in Israel.

Wisdom motifs found their way into Israelite psalms at an early period. For instance, Psalm 78, one of the "salvation history" psalms to which we have alluded several times, begins in the style of a wisdom poem (vss. 1-4). In verse 2 the recitation of Yahweh's deeds and the people's unfaithfulness is specifically called a wisdom utterance (*mashal*, Hebrew; "parable," RSV). The purpose of the psalm is to edify the congregation through the recollection of history, so that the people may learn from the past how to live in the present. The introduction to this psalm is like the opening of Psalm 49, in which a wisdom meditation upon the transience of life (compare Psalm 90) is brought into the context of worship.

Hear this, all peoples!
> Give ear, all inhabitants of the world,
both low and high,
> rich and poor together!
My mouth shall speak wisdom;
> the meditation of my heart shall be understanding.
I will incline my ear to a proverb (mashal);
> I will solve my riddle to the music of the lyre.
> > —Psalm 49:1-4

These psalms show that the Israelite faith did not advocate a "sacrifice of the intellect"—such as is made in some situations today where a person leaves his intellect, along with his coat and hat, in the vestibule before entering the sanctuary! Wisdom, rather, belongs in the context of worship, as attested by the presence of wisdom psalms in the Psalter.

WISDOM PSALMS

36 "With thee is the fountain of life" (This psalm contains elements of the lament and hymn.)

*37 "Be still before Yahweh, and wait patiently for him"

*49 "The meditation of my heart shall be understanding"

*73 "Nevertheless I am continually with thee"

78 "I will open my mouth in a parable"
(salvation history psalm)

112 "Blessed is the man who fears Yahweh"

127 "Unless Yahweh builds the house . . ."

128 "Blessed is every one who fears Yahweh"

133 "How good and pleasant it is when brothers dwell in unity!"

(See also Proverbs 8; Ecclesiasticus 14:20-15:10.)

These psalms are not immediately and essentially connected with specific acts of worship, and therefore may be considered non-cultic. Although they refer to going to the sanctuary (Ps. 73:17) or use the metaphor of finding refuge under Yahweh's wings (36:7)—a reference to the wings of the cherubim outstretched over the Ark in the Holy of Holies—they are essentially meditations on the good life. Often they begin with beatitudes ("blessed [happy] is the man who . . .") or contain admonitions against following evil and foolish ways. The ultimate background of this instruction is the ancient doctrine of the Two Ways as taught in wisdom circles: the way of life which the wise pursue and the way of destruction which the foolish follow (cf. Matt. 7:13-14). According to Israel's faith, however, this instruction does not have its source in human wisdom; rather, it is a divine gift. Yahweh teaches men to walk in "the right paths," the paths of salvation. Accordingly, in Israel's wisdom psalms true wisdom is identified with "the fear of Yahweh" and, even more specifically, with faithfulness to his *torah* ("teaching," "instruction"; often weakly translated, "law"). One of the stanzas in Psalm 37, which is based on the alphabetical acrostic pattern, says:

The mouth of the righteous utters wisdom,
   and his tongue speaks justice.
The law (torah) of his God is in his heart;
   his steps do not slip.
                    —Psalm 37:30-31

Several psalms extol Yahweh's *torah* (teaching) as the basis of true wisdom and happiness.

TORAH PSALMS

   *1 "On his law he meditates day and night"
   *19 (7-14) "The law of Yahweh is perfect"
   119 "Blessed are those who walk in the law of Yahweh!"

Of these psalms the best known is Psalm 1, which opens the Psalter with the beatitude typical of a wisdom poem ("Blessed . . ."). The wise man is the one who meditates on Yahweh's teaching, found preeminently in the first five books of the Old Testament, known in Jewish tradition as "The Torah" (Greek, *Pentateuch*). He is like a tree, whose roots are nourished by a life-giving stream, in contrast to the wicked who are like evanescent chaff, driven away by the wind. The wise (righteous) man is secure, contented, and prosperous. This theme, which is developed with chaste simplicity in Psalm 1, is expanded to almost wearisome length in Psalm 119, the longest psalm in the Psalter. The only unity Psalm 119 has is that of the Hebrew alphabet: each successive stanza begins with the next letter of the alphabet. This acrostic pattern is also followed in two of the wisdom psalms (Pss. 37 and 112).* This alphabetical scheme was a convenient device for teaching or memorizing, but psalms of this kind are far removed from those shaped by liturgical usage or even those that imitated cultic forms.

THE ENIGMAS OF LIFE

The wisdom and torah psalms, despite their differences, agree on one premise: the man who fears Yahweh is "happy," the ungodly man is denied this felicity. Of course, the term "happy" has been weakened by the superficial meanings of our society, and in this context it may be best to retain the older word "blessed" with its strong biblical flavor. In any case, these psalms give the assurance that the man who fears Yahweh and obeys his teaching will enjoy the good life—not in another world, but in this historical world, here and now. Man's relationship with God will mean the enjoyment of God and hence the enjoyment of life. Such a man will experience all that "salvation" involves: health, wholeness, welfare, the freedom to be, and to serve God, in the covenant community.

It is this healthy, life-affirming attitude, however, which prompts the question with which these wisdom

---

* Besides Psalms 37, 112, and 119 the following Psalms are alphabetical acrostics: Psalms 9-10, 25, 34, 111, 145.

psalms wrestle: why is it that things often work out so badly for the God-fearing man and so well for the person who is careless about, or defiant of, God? Three wisdom psalms, 37, 49, and 73, are especially concerned with this problem—one which has plagued men of faith down through the centuries. Beyond the Psalter the Book of Job is preeminently addressed to this problem.[7]

The simple solution to the problem—the one advanced by friends of Job—was to say that life's imbalances are only temporary and will be rectified shortly. In the meantime, suffering is, at best, the chastening or correction of the Almighty (Job 5:17-27). Yet one has only to read Psalm 37 to realize that this kind of answer is a whistling in the dark. Here the psalmist goes all the way with the doctrine: just be patient and you will see the reward of the righteous and the retribution of the wicked. Indeed, at one point he blandly testifies:

I have been young, and now am old;
> **yet I have not seen the righteous forsaken**
> **or his children begging bread.**
>> **—Psalm 37:25**

The appropriate response to this statement is that the psalmist either had not lived long enough, or that he must have lived someplace where he was sheltered from the hard realities of life! Furthermore, the possibility has to be reckoned with—as at the end of the book of Job —that suffering *may* be the occasion for a deeper understanding of man's relation to God.

Psalm 73, the greatest of the wisdom psalms, grapples with this problem at the profoundest level in the whole Psalter, and in so doing comes closest to the book of Job. The psalmist begins by asserting the "orthodox" thesis:

Truly God is good to the upright,
**   to those who are pure in heart.**
**   —Psalm 73:1**

Then follows the crucial "but" (vs. 2)—the "adversative conjunction"—which was dictated by the psalmist's own experience. When he considered the imbalances of life, he says, his faith was almost destroyed (vss. 2-16). The only thing that restrained him from speaking out his doubts was his concern for the effect that it would have on the younger generation!

Searching for an answer to this baffling problem was a "wearisome task," and the psalmist confesses that he was about to surrender his faith:

until I went into the sanctuary of God;
**   then I perceived their end.**
Truly thou dost set them in slippery places;
**   thou dost make them fall to ruin.**
How they are destroyed in a moment,
**   swept away utterly by terrors!**
They are like a dream when one awakes,
**   on awaking you despise their phantoms.**
**   —Psalm 73:17-20**

Like Job, the psalmist was ready to recant his presumptuous attempt to judge the ways of God from the limited standpoint of his experience (cf. Job 42:1-6). But, like Job, he too seemed to break through the limitations of his past understanding into a new apprehension of God's presence and power, which his theology, however orthodox, could not fully comprehend. The turning point in the psalm is indicated by another "adversative conjunction"—"the great nevertheless" which stands at the beginning of verse 23:

Nevertheless I am continually with thee;
 thou dost hold my right hand.
Thou dost guide me with thy counsel,
 and afterward thou wilt receive me to glory.
—Psalm 73:23-24

The meaning of the last sentence, unfortunately, is obscure in the Hebrew. It may be, as some interpreters have insisted, one of the few places in the Old Testament where there is an "intimation of immortality," that is, a hope for a breakthrough into a new form of existence in which, as Paul put it, "the mortal puts on immortality" in a mystery which is comprehended solely in God's grace (I Cor. 15:42-58). But if it is an intimation, it is no more. The psalmist is not really concerned with what lies beyond the boundary of death, but with the solution to existential problems which *now* demand an answer if man is to live in faith, and die in faith.

This psalm speaks directly to us in the theological bewilderment of the 20th century—not because it gives a theological answer, but because it portrays the situation in which new theological formulations must be found. Today we know, even more radically than the wisdom psalmist, that theological formulations which were satisfactory in a previous day no longer cope with the hard realities of contemporary human experience. How can one talk about the "happiness" of men of faith in a world where six million Jews were burned in Nazi ovens, where many people are doomed to live out their lives in economic ghettos, where the threat of atomic annihilation hangs over every military adventure, where man's science is pushing back our historical horizons into the vast reaches of the cosmos? Theology that is vital stands on the boundary between the old theology which has been systematized and the new theology which must be formulated. And if man's intellect is to be brought into the sanctuary of God, this standing on the boundary between the old and the new is imperative.

READING THE PSALMS IN THE CHRIST-CONTEXT

We return, then, to the question which was raised at the outset of this study: In what sense does the Psalter speak to us of Jesus Christ? The New Testament wrestles with this question in various passages, by saying that the Psalms not only anticipate the advent of the King who would inaugurate God's kingdom but portray the passion and struggle he would go through in fulfilling his task. Today we can say with greater clarity that the whole history of Israel, from the oppression in Egypt and on, was a passion story in which Israel experienced the reality of God in the midst of suffering, a suffering which—as the prophet Second Isaiah perceived—was borne vicariously in order that the nations and the whole creation might rejoice in the God who is Creator and Lord. The Psalms show, as Christoph Barth observes, that "Jesus and Israel belong together, and that their respective histories cannot be understood apart from each other." [8] From the Christian point of view the history of Jesus and the history of Israel constitute *one* history: the history in which God makes himself present in the midst of his people to open a way into the future when there is no way.

Psalm 73, as we have noticed, reaches a turning point in "the great nevertheless." This is not an adversative which turns man away from the problems of existence; rather, it turns man toward the world with the confidence that God is present and at work there. In its simplest terms this faith affirms: "Nevertheless, I am continually with thee." On a profounder level this Biblical faith joyfully announces that, because of God's victory in

Jesus Christ, "in all these things we are more than conquerors through him who loved us":

> For I am sure that neither death, nor life, nor angels,
> nor principalities, nor things present, nor things to
> come, nor powers, nor height, nor depth, nor anything
> else in all creation, will be able to separate us from
> the love of God in Christ Jesus our Lord.
>
> —Romans 8:38-39

This means that, as Bonhoeffer has emphasized, there is no suffering in which Christ is not with us—suffering with us, praying with us, triumphing with us. Such a faith, which is ever open to new theological formulations, enables men to join in the singing of the laments, the thanksgivings, and the hymns of the Psalter, in the name of Christ and to the glory of God.

APPENDIX A: *Outline of Psalms*
Considered in
This Study

(Asterisks mark psalms recommended for special reading. Some psalms are listed in more than one place.)

Chapter 2: Salvation History Psalms

*78	135
*105	*136
106	

Chapter 3: Laments

COMMUNITY LAMENTS

*12	*85
*44	*90
58	*94
60	123
74	126
79	129
*80	137
83	Lamentations 5

INDIVIDUAL LAMENTS

*3	54
*4 (song of trust?)	55
5	56
7	*57
9-10	59
13	61
14 (= 53)	64
17	69
*22	70 (= 40:13-17)
25	*71
26	*77
27:7-14	86
28	88
*31	89 (royal lament)
35	109
*39	120
40:12-17	*139
41	140
*42-43	141
52	142
53 (= 14)	Lamentations 3

PENITENTIAL PSALMS

6	*102
32 (song of thanks)	*130
*38	*143
*51	

Chapter 4: Songs of Thanksgiving

COMMUNITY SONGS OF THANKSGIVING

65 (hymn?)	*124
67 (hymn?)	136 (hymn?)
75	I Samuel 2:1-10
*107	

INDIVIDUAL SONGS OF THANKSGIVING

18 (= II Sam. 22)	*92
(royal thanksgiving)	*116
30	*118 (royal thanksgiving)
*32 (penitential psalm)	*138
*34	Isaiah 38:9-20
40:1-11	Jonah 2:2-9
66:13-20	

Chapter 5: Hymns of Praise

HYMNS TO THE CREATOR OF THE UNIVERSE ("CREATION PSALMS")

*8	*104
*19:1-6	*148

HYMNS TO THE GOD WHO CREATED AND CHOSE ISRAEL

66:1-12	149
*100	Exodus 15:1-18
111	Deuteronomy 32:1-43
114	Habakkuk 3:2-19

HYMNS TO THE CREATOR AS LORD OF HISTORY

*33	*145
*103	*146
113	*147
117	

DOXOLOGY

150

Chapter 6: Festival Songs and Liturgies

COVENANT-RENEWAL LITURGIES
50
*81

PSALMS OF THE DAVIDIC COVENANT
*78 (salvation history psalm)
*89 (royal lament)
*132

ROYAL PSALMS
*2
72
*18 (royal thanksgiving)
101
20
*110
21
144:1-11 (royal lament)
45

SONGS OF ZION
*46
*84
48
87
76
*122

ENTHRONEMENT PSALMS
24 (entrance liturgy)
96
29
97
*47
*98
93
99
*95

Chapter 7: Songs of Trust and Meditation

SONGS OF TRUST
11
*63 (individual lament?)
16
*91
*23
*121
*27:1-6
125 (community lament?)
62
131

WISDOM PSALMS
36 (mixed type)
127
*37
128
*49
133
*73
Proverbs 8
78 (salvation history)
Ecclesiasticus 14:20-15:10
112

TORAH PSALMS
*1
*19:7-14
119

Psalms not included in the above outline:

LITURGIES

15 (compare Ps. 24)	115
68	134
82	

MIXED TYPES

108

APPENDIX B: *Index of Psalms*
According to Type

The following is presented only as a working basis for the study of the Psalms. There are too many uncertainties to permit an exact and rigid classification according to type.

Psalm	Type
BOOK I	
1	Torah (wisdom) psalm
2	Royal psalm
3	Individual lament
4	Individual lament (psalm of trust?)
5	Individual lament
6	Individual lament (penitential psalm)
7	Individual lament
8	Hymn
9-10	Individual lament? (alphabetical acrostic)
11	Song of trust
12	Community lament
13	Individual lament
14	(= 53) Individual lament
15	Liturgy for admission to the cult
16	Song of trust
17	Individual lament
18	(= II Sam. 22) Individual thanksgiving (royal)
19:1-6	Hymn
19:7-14	Torah (wisdom) psalm
20	Royal psalm
21	Royal psalm
22	Individual lament
23	Song of trust
24	Hymn
25	Individual lament (alphabetical acrostic)
26	Individual lament

Psalm	Type
27:1-6	Song of trust
27:7-14	Individual lament
28	Individual lament
29	Hymn
30	Individual song of thanksgiving
31	Individual lament
32	Individual song of thanksgiving (penitential psalm)
33	Hymn
34	Individual song of thanksgiving (alphabetical acrostic)
35	Individual lament
36	Wisdom psalm (including lament, hymn)
37	Wisdom psalm (alphabetical acrostic)
38	Individual lament (penitential psalm)
39	Individual lament
40:1-11	Individual song of thanksgiving
40:12-17	Individual lament
41	Individual lament

BOOK II

42-43	Individual lament
44	Community lament
45	Royal psalm
46	Song of Zion
47	Hymn
48	Song of Zion
49	Wisdom psalm
50	Covenant-renewal liturgy
51	Individual lament (penitential psalm)
52	Individual lament (mixture of types)
53	(= 14) Individual lament
54	Individual lament
55	Individual lament
56	Individual lament
57	Individual lament
58	Community lament

Psalm	Type
59	Individual lament
60	Community lament
61	Individual lament
62	Song of trust
63	Song of trust (individual lament?)
64	Individual lament
65	Community song of thanksgiving (hymn?)
66:1-12	Hymn
66:13-20	Individual song of thanksgiving
67	Community song of thanksgiving (hymn?)
68	Zion liturgy (?)
69	Individual lament
70	(= 40:13-17) Individual lament
71	Individual lament
72	Royal psalm

BOOK III

Psalm	Type
73	Wisdom psalm
74	Community lament
75	Community song of thanksgiving (?)
76	Song of Zion
77	Individual lament
78	Salvation history psalm (wisdom psalm?)
79	Community lament
80	Community lament
81	Covenant renewal liturgy
82	Liturgy
83	Community lament
84	Song of Zion
85	Community lament
86	Individual lament
87	Song of Zion
88	Individual lament
89	Individual lament (royal)

BOOK IV

Psalm	Type
90	Community lament

Psalm	Type
91	Song of trust
92	Individual song of thanksgiving
93	Hymn
94	Community lament
95	Hymn
96	Hymn
97	Hymn
98	Hymn
99	Hymn
100	Hymn
101	Royal psalm
102	Individual lament including hymnic elements (penitential)
103	Hymn
104	Hymn
105	Salvation history psalm (hymn)
106	Salvation history psalm

BOOK V

Psalm	Type
107	Community song of thanksgiving
108	(= 57:7-11; 60:5-12) Mixed type
109	Individual lament
110	Royal psalm
111	Hymn (alphabetical acrostic)
112	Wisdom psalm (alphabetical acrostic)
113	Hymn
114	Hymn
115	Liturgy
116	Individual song of thanksgiving
117	Hymn
118	Individual song of thanksgiving (royal)
119	Torah (wisdom) psalm (alphabetical acrostic)
120	Individual lament
121	Song of trust
122	Song of Zion
123	Community lament

Psalm	Type
124	Community song of thanksgiving
125	Song of trust (community lament?)
126	Community lament (?)
127	Wisdom psalm
128	Wisdom psalm
129	Community lament (?)
130	Individual lament (penitential psalm)
131	Song of trust
132	Liturgy of the Davidic covenant
133	Wisdom psalm
134	Liturgy
135	Salvation history psalm (hymn)
136	Salvation history psalm (hymn; community thanksgiving?)
137	Community lament
138	Individual song of thanksgiving
139	Individual lament (wisdom psalm?)
140	Individual lament
141	Individual lament
142	Individual lament
143	Individual lament
144:1-11	Royal psalm
145	Hymn (alphabetical acrostic)
146	Hymn
147	Hymn
148	Hymn
149	Hymn
150	Doxology to conclude the Psalter

NOTES *

CHAPTER 1: *The Psalms and the Worshiping Community*

1. Claus Westermann, *The Praise of God in the Psalms*, trans. Keith R. Crim (Richmond, Va.: John Knox Press, 1965), p. 10.

2. John D. Godsey summarizes Bonhoeffer's book in *The Theology of Dietrich Bonhoeffer* (Philadelphia: The Westminster Press, 1960; © W. L. Jenkins, 1960), pp. 189-94. Used by permission.

3. Amos N. Wilder, *The Language of the Gospel* (New York: Harper & Row, 1964), chap. 1, especially p. 24.

4. Christoph Barth, *Introduction to the Psalms*, trans. R. A. Wilson (New York: Chas. Scribner's Sons, 1966), p. 75.

5. W. T. Davison: "More than any other book of the Old Testament it [the Psalter] has been baptized into Christ." Quoted by John Paterson, *The Praises of. Israel* (New York: Scribner's, 1950), p. 7.

6. See, for instance, T. H. Gaster, *The Dead Sea Scriptures* (New York: Doubleday, Anchor, 1956), pp. 123-202. The archaeological discovery of the Qumran library began in 1947.

7. Deviations from the Hebrew tradition of the Psalter are discussed by J. A. Sanders, *The Dead Sea Psalms Scroll* (Ithaca, N.Y.: Cornell University Press, 1967).

8. Two of the psalms in the first Davidic collection, Pss. 10 and 33, are not explicitly ascribed to David. Ps. 10, however, is actually the second half of an alphabetical psalm, i.e., one in which every second verse begins with a successive letter of the Hebrew alphabet. The first half of the alphabetical sequence is Ps. 9 (ascribed to David), and thus Pss. 9 and 10 should be considered one psalm, as in the Greek Old Testament (Septuagint). The other psalm in question, Ps. 33, is ascribed to David in the Septuagint.

9. Artur Weiser, *The Psalms: A Commentary*, trans. Herbert Hartwell (Phila.: The Westminster Press, 1962; © SCM Press, 1962), p. 96. Used by permission.

10. Christoph Barth, *Introduction to the Psalms*, pp. 64-65.

11. Hermann Gunkel's monumental work, *Einleitung in die Psal-*

---

* NOTE: *Grateful acknowledgement is made of quoted materials, which are used by permission.* Editor.

men (2nd ed., 1933) has not yet been translated; however, an essay in which he classifies psalms according to type is available: *The Psalms: A Form-Critical Introduction,* Facet Books (Philadelphia: Fortress Press, 1967).

For Sigmund Mowinckel's study of the cultic situation of the psalms see *The Psalms in Israel's Worship* (Nashville: Abingdon Press, 1962).

CHAPTER 2: *Enthroned on the Praises of Israel*

1. *The Confessions of Saint Augustine,* trans. J. G. Pilkington (New York: Liveright Publishing Corp., 1943), Book 1, chap. 1.

2. "Hymn to the Moon-God," translated by Ferris J. Stephens, in *Ancient Near Eastern Texts Relating to the Old Testament,* 3rd ed., edited by J. B. Pritchard (Princeton: Princeton University Press, 1969), p. 385 f. In this hymn the "Igigi" are the great gods of heaven; the "Anunnaki" are the gods of the earth and the netherworld.

3. "Hymn to the Aton," translated by John A. Wilson, *Ancient Near Eastern Texts,* ed., J. B. Pritchard, pp. 369-73.

4. These lines are influenced by a paper presented by Arthur C. McGill on "A Theological Criticism of 'Transcendence,'" at the Society of the Biblical Theologians, November 17, 1967.

5. See further Bernhard W. Anderson, *Creation versus Chaos* (New York: Association Press, 1967), chap. 1 on "Creation and History."

6. Amos Wilder, *The Language of the Gospel* (New York: Harper & Row, 1964), p. 64 f.

7. The reading preferably should be done with the aid of *The Oxford Annotated Bible with the Apocrypha,* edited by Herber G. May and Bruce M. Metzger (New York: Oxford University Press, 1965).

8. The hallelujah at the end of Psalm 104 actually belongs at the beginning of Psalm 105. Psalm 135 is also a hallelujah psalm, while Psalm 136 is a *todah* ("thanksgiving") psalm, as is clear from its beginning and end.

9. H. Richard Niebuhr, *The Meaning of Revelation* (New York: The Macmillan Co., 1941), p. 48.

10. Helmer Ringgren, *The Faith of the Psalmists* (Philadelphia: Fortress Press, 1963), p. 35.

CHAPTER 3: *Murmurings in the Absence of God*

1. Claus Westermann points out that, in contrast to Babylonian psalms, "something entirely new has been added to the psalms of praise in the Old Testament: the imperative exhortation to praise." Claus Westermann, *The Praise of God in the Psalms*, trans. Keith R. Crim (Richmond, Va.: John Knox Press, 1965), p. 37.

2. Translated by Ferris J. Stephens in *Ancient Near Eastern Texts*, ed., J. B. Pritchard, pp. 383-85.

3. Theodor H. Gaster, *The Dead Sea Scriptures* (New York: Doubleday & Co., 1956), p. 112. Gaster objects to the prosaic interpretation of the enemies in these psalms ("the company of Belial," "the men of corruption") as adversaries escaped or overcome in warfare. Such a view, he remarks, "confuses the 'slings and arrows of outrageous fortune' with concrete bazookas and guided missiles."

4. Christoph Barth, *Introduction to the Psalms*, trans. R. A. Wilson (New York: Chas. Scribner's Sons, 1966), p. 38.

5. Helmer Ringgren's brief discussion of "The Psalms and Comparative Religion," in *The Faith of the Psalmists* (Philadelphia: Fortress Press, 1963), pp. 115-21, is helpful in this connection.

6. Bonhoeffer's view is expressed by John Godsey in *The Theology of Dietrich Bonhoeffer* (Philadelphia: The Westminster Press, 1960; © W. L. Jenkins, 1960), p. 191. Christoph Barth expresses Bonhoeffer's view in his discussion of the "wicked enemies" in *Introduction to the Psalms*, p. 43.

7. Helmer Ringgren, *The Faith of the Psalmists*, p. 45 (see also pp. 44-46). This theme is discussed in Bernhard W. Anderson, *Creation versus Chaos* (New York: Association Press, 1967); see especially chap. 5 on "Creation and Conflict."

8. This phrase is quoted by James H. Smylie in his article, "On Jesus, Pharaoh, and the Chosen People: Martin Luther King as Biblical Interpreter and Humanist," *Interpretation*, XXIV, 1 (January 1970), p. 78.

9. G. Ernest Wright, "Reflections concerning Old Testament Theology," in *Studia Biblica et Semitica*, edited by Theodore C. Vriezen (The Netherlands: H. Veenman en Zonen, 1966), p. 387.

10. Claus Westermann, *A Thousand Years and a Day* (Philadelphia: Fortress Press, 1962), p. 268. See also Helmer Ringgren, *The Faith of the Psalmists*, pp. 31-32.

11. Dietrich Bonhoeffer, according to John Godsey, in *The Theology of Dietrich Bonhoeffer*, p. 193.

    See also in this connection the illuminating discussion by Christoph Barth of "righteous sinners" and "wicked enemies," in *Introduction to the Psalms*, pp. 39-42 and 43-48.

12. Christoph Barth, *Introduction to the Psalms*, p. 42. Note that in Jesus' parable of the Pharisee and the Publican (Luke 18:9-14), it is the Publican—a sinner—who is declared to be in right relationship with God, that is, "justified."

13. Wayne C. Richards, from "Psalms of Silence: Contemporary Laments" (1966; unpublished); used by permission and with deep appreciation.

CHAPTER 4: *Taste and See That the Lord Is Good!*

1. Dietrich Bonhoeffer, *Prisoner for God: Letters and Papers from Prison* (New York: The Macmillan Co., 1960), pp. 32-33. Bonhoeffer was hanged on April 9, 1945, for his part in a conspiracy against Hitler.

2. Sigismund Payne Best in *The Venlo Incident* (London: Hutchinson Publishing Group, 1950), cited by Eberhard Baethge in the preface to Dietrich Bonhoeffer's *Prisoner for God*, p. 11.

3. Otto Eissfeldt, *The Old Testament: an Introduction* (New York: Harper & Row, 1965), p. 122. He concludes: "Thus the Phoenician cultus, too, was familiar with the gesture of thanksgiving which the psalm passage attests [Ps. 116:13], and the words quoted from the inscription lead to the surmise that there existed there, too, songs of thanksgiving similar to those of the Old Testament, as we have similar ones in Egypt in fair numbers and in fact from a very early date."

    The Phoenician inscription is found in *Ancient Near Eastern Texts*, ed., J. B. Pritchard, p. 502; an example of an Egyptian inscription in "Gratitude for God's Mercy" is found on p. 380 f.

4. James M. Robinson discusses the genre of the "thanksgiving" and the "blessing," both of which appear prominently in the Qumran psalms, in his essay on biblical language which appears in *The Old Testament and Christian Faith*, edited by Bernhard W. Anderson (New York: Herder & Herder, 1969), especially p. 131 ff.

5. See the important monograph by the British scholar, Aubrey R. Johnson, *The Vitality of the Individual in the Thought of Ancient Israel* (Cardiff: University of Wales Press, 1949).

Another fundamental study is the work by the Scandinavian scholar Johannes Pedersen, *Israel: its Life and Culture*, I-II, III-IV (London: Oxford University Press, 1926-1940); see especially I-II, pp. 453-496.

6. See further Bernhard W. Anderson, *Creation versus Chaos* (New York: Association Press, 1967), especially pp. 93-99.

7. In this connection the penetrating discussion of "The Power and Overthrow of Death" by Christoph Barth, *Introduction to the Psalms*, trans. R. A. Wilson (New York: Chas. Scribner's Sons, 1966), pp. 49-55, merits careful reading.

8. Christoph Barth, *Introduction to the Psalms*, pp. 50f., 54f. In this context he observes: " 'Life' for the psalms means the historical formation and appearance of the people of God, while 'death' means their sinking back into the natural existence of the heathen, fundamentally without history."

9. Dietrich Bonhoeffer, *Prisoner for God: Letters and Papers from Prison*, p. 79.

CHAPTER 5: *How Majestic Is Thy Name in All the Earth!*

1. Hermann Gunkel, *What Remains of the Old Testament*, trans. K. Dallas (New York: The Macmillan Co., 1928; © Copyright Geo. Allen & Unwin, Ltd.), p. 70f.

2. Otto Eissfeldt, *The Old Testament: An Introduction* (New York: Harper & Row, 1965), p. 105f.

3. Helmer Ringgren, in his study *The Faith of the Psalmists* (Philadelphia: Fortress Press, 1963), emphasizes this aspect of visual participation in the ritual drama: "The creation and the exodus from Egypt were not only great and precious memories treasured by the faithful and now and then recollected or commemorated. They were events that were actualized and re-experienced whenever the great festivals were celebrated in the temple," p. 90. See also the ensuing discussion.

4. The concluding hallelujah ("Praise Yahweh") is sometimes regarded as the beginning of the following Psalm 118, as in the Greek translation of the Old Testament. But such a con-

clusion is found at the end of Pss. 104, 105, 106, 113, 115, 116, and in this case, too, is probably a formal part of the psalm. The first verse of the psalm is quoted in Romans 15:11.

5. Some of these ancient hymns are found in *Ancient Near Eastern Texts*, ed. J. B. Pritchard, pp. 365-401.

6. See the discussion of "Name" by Johannes Pedersen in *Israel: Its Life and Culture, I, II* (London: Oxford University Press, 1926, 1959), pp. 245-59.

7. Translated by the Revised Standard Version as "I AM WHO I AM" (Ex. 3:14). An illuminating discussion of this passage and the whole question of the name of God is given by Gerhard von Rad in his little book, *Moses*, World Christian Books (New York: Association Press, 1960), chap. 2.

8. See Gerhard von Rad, *Old Testament Theology*, I (New York: Harper & Row, 1962), p. 362.

9. Contrast Joseph Addison's (1672-1719) hymn, "The Spacious Firmament on High," which declares that "in reason's ear" the anthem of nature is heard. The hymn reflects the rationalism of the Enlightenment. Blaise Pascal (1623-1662) spoke more authentically for the modern mind when he confessed that he was torn between evidences of the Creator in nature and evidences from nature which negated his faith. See his *Pensées*, The Modern Library (New York: Random House, 1941), Fragment 229.

10. On the hymns of creation, see further Bernhard W. Anderson, *Creation versus Chaos* (New York: Association Press, 1967), chap. 3 on "Creation and Worship."

11. The word 'Elohim in verse 5 may refer to the heavenly beings or "sons of God" who, according to the ancient pictorial way of thinking, surround God in his heavenly court. This view seems to be presupposed in Gen. 1:26, where the plural forms ("Let us . . . in our image") suggest that God is addressing his heavenly council (cf. I Kings 22:19). The Greek translation of the Old Testament reads "angels" at Ps. 8:5, and this interpretation is adopted in the Epistle to the Hebrews where the psalm is quoted (Heb. 2:5-9).

12. Notice that in Gen. 5:3 the terms "image" and "likeness" are used to describe the relationship between Adam and Seth, father and son. The son is the image of his father, which indicates not only resemblance but a relationship which constitutes the son.

13. Mircea Eliade, *Cosmos and History: the Myth of the Eternal Return* (New York: Harper & Row, 1959), p. 34. The entire book is an illuminating study of archaic religions. See also

my discussion of the mythical view of reality in *Creation versus Chaos*, pp. 26-33.

CHAPTER 6: *Thine Is the Kingdom*

1. See the valuable chapter on "The Cultic Element" in Helmer Ringgren's *The Faith of the Psalmists* (Philadelphia: Fortress Press, 1963), chap. 1. He writes: "The psalms were not written for private use—at least, not originally, but for use in the cult of the Yahweh community, and in most cases the cult of the preexilic community" (p. 1).

2. See Walter Harrelson, *Interpreting the Old Testament* (New York: Holt, Rinehart and Winston, Inc., 1964), p. 122.

3. See *The Book of Worship* of The [United] Methodist Church, pp. 382-88.

4. Artur Weiser, in *The Psalms: a Commentary*, trans. Herbert Hartwell (Philadelphia: The Westminster Press, 1962; © SCM Press Ltd., 1962), assigns a great number of psalms to the festival of covenant renewal, but he clearly goes too far. Many of the psalms so classified belong to the Zion festival, which emphasized God's covenant with David and his choice of Zion. See the subsequent discussion in this chapter.

5. The Sumerian king list, dating back to the third millennium B.C., is found in *Ancient Near Eastern Texts*, ed., J. B. Pritchard, p. 265.

6. In this connection Christoph Barth remarks that in Israelite tradition, particularly in the books of Samuel and Kings, "this kingdom is rooted in what had been begun centuries earlier, and had been constantly renewed ever since, the choosing, gathering together and separation of Israel as the property, first-born-child, people and worshiping community of their God." Christoph Barth, *Introduction to the Psalms*, trans. R. A. Wilson (New York: Chas. Scribner's Sons, 1966), p. 23.

7. See Mircea Eliade's discussion of "The Symbolism of the Center" in *Cosmos and History* (New York: Harper & Row, 1959), pp. 12-17.

8. See Sigmund Mowinckel, *The Psalms in Israel's Worship*, I-II (Nashville: Abingdon Press, 1962), especially I, chap. 5, "Psalms at the Enthronement Festival of Yahweh," pp. 106-192. Mowinckel's thesis is discussed in my book, *Creation versus Chaos* (New York: Association Press, 1967), chap. 3.

CHAPTER 7: *A Table Prepared*

1. Aage Bentzen, *Introduction to the Old Testament*, II, 4th ed. (Copenhagen: G.E.C. Gads Forlag, 1958), p. 170. Bentzen observes: "The Book of Psalms is not only a ritual song book, but also, and perhaps more, a 'Wisdom Book,' a book showing the way of a righteous life."

2. Also Pss. 13:5; 52:8; 73:23; 141:8. This "adversative conjunction" is discussed by Claus Westermann, *The Praise of God in the Psalms* (Richmond, Va.: John Knox Press, 1965), pp. 70-75.

3. Comment on Psalm 27:4 by Artur Weiser, *The Psalms: a Commentary*, trans. Herbert Hartwell (Philadelphia: The Westminster Press, 1962; © SCM Press Ltd., 1962), p. 248.

4. At this point the author's translation follows some versions reading "and I dwell," rather than the received Hebrew text, "and I return." Here the idea is not that of taking up residence permanently in the temple, but rather, as in Ps. 15:1, being a guest or sojourner in Yahweh's "tent"—that is, frequently visiting the holy place where God is present. In vs. 4 the author has adopted the translation "they reassure me" from the Jewish scholar, Julius Morgenstern. On oil as a symbol of festive joy (vs. 5), see Pss. 45:7; 92:10-11; 133:2.

5. This interpretation is influenced by John Paterson's exposition of Psalm 23 in *The Praises of Israel* (New York: Chas. Scribner's Sons, 1950), pp. 108-115, which in turn depends upon a study by George Adam Smith.

6. Artur Weiser, *The Psalms: a Commentary*, p. 227.

7. See the discussion of the Book of Job in Bernhard W. Anderson, *Understanding the Old Testament*, 2nd. ed. (Englewood Cliffs, N.J.: Prentice-Hall, 1966), pp. 506-518.

8. Christoph Barth, *Introduction to the Psalms*, trans. R. A. Wilson (New York: Chas. Scribner's Sons, 1966), p. 70.

NOTE: Biblical quotations are from the *Revised Standard Version of the Bible*. The author, however, has chosen to use the Hebrew term "Yahweh" rather than "the Lord" which appears in the *Revised Standard Version. Editor.*

GLOSSARY

ACROSTIC—A composition in which the initial letters of sentences or stanzas form a pattern, such as the sequence of the alphabet.

ACTUALIZE—A verb used in current biblical studies to indicate the act of making the past present, contemporizing the tradition—as in the sacrament of Holy Communion when the event of the Crucifixion is re-experienced or reenacted.

AD HOMINEM—"To the man"; of an argument directed at one's prejudices rather than one's intellect.

ADVERSATIVE—Expressing opposition, contrariety, or antithesis.

ANACHRONISTIC—Out of its proper place in time; especially dating from a period earlier than the actual period.

ANTIPHONAL—The singing of a verse in response, particularly a psalm, hymn, or prayer sung in alternate parts.

APOCRYPHA—In Protestant usage this refers to a collection of writings, not found in the Hebrew Bible, which gained great prestige in the period of the early church and which in the Roman Catholic and Eastern Orthodox church are regarded as part of the Old Testament.

ARCHETYPE—A fundamental, basic pattern or model, of which other related things or ideas may be regarded as copies or representations. In ancient Babylonia, for instance, it was believed that the heavenly temple was the archetype after which the earthly temple was modeled. (See prototype.)

BABYLONIA, BABYLONIAN—The people who, under Hammurabi, established a great empire with Babylon as capital in the early second millennium B.C. In the seventh century B.C. this empire revived and subjugated Palestine.

BEDOUIN—A nomadic Arab of the desert in Asia or Africa.

CHAOS, WATERS OF—In ancient mythology (e.g., Babylonian) the waters (Sea, Deep, Floods) stand for the powers of evil and confusion which the Creator defeated in the beginning but which continue to reassert their hostility to the divine rule.

CHERUB, CHERUBIM (plural)—In the Old Testament cherubim were regarded as superhuman beings who guard sacred areas, such as Eden (Gen. 3:24), or the Holy of Holies in the Temple (I Kings 6:23-29). In ancient Babylonia and Assyria such guardian figures (represented as winged lions with human heads) were placed at the entrance to palaces and temples.

CHRISTOLOGY, CHRISTOLOGICAL—Pertaining to the branch of theology that deals with the person, teaching, and work of Christ.

CONSUMMATION—Completion, fulfillment, perfection.

COSMOS—The idea of the universe as an orderly and harmonious system.

COVENANT—A term drawn from ancient political life (related to "treaty") which describes a voluntary agreement or relationship entered into between a superior power and a subordinate people. This political terminology was appropriated to express the relation between God and his people, Israel.

CULT, CULTIC—The rites and beliefs connected with the worship of God, viewed as an interrelated whole; thus, the *way* man worships; an order of worship, or liturgical form.

CULTUS—Established or accepted rites of worship; cult.

DEAD SEA SCROLLS—Writings belonging to the monastic Jewish community which flourished on the western shore of the Dead Sea from about 100 B.C. until its destruction by the Romans in the second century A.D. The library of this sectarian group was discovered in caves near the Dead Sea, beginning in 1947.

DIDACHE—"Teaching of the Twelve Apostles"; a Christian manual of the early second century dealing with Christian morals and worship, by an unknown author.

DIDACTIC—Intended to teach or instruct.

DIVINER—One who attempts to foretell the future or penetrate the unknown through occult means.

DOXOLOGY—An ascription of praise to God. The word is based on a Greek compound which includes the elements "glory, praise," plus "speak"—thus, to "speak praise." [See Hallelujah.]

ECCLESIASTICUS—One of the writings found in the "Apocrypha," alternatively known as the Wisdom of Jesus ben Sirach and not to be confused with the biblical book of Ecclesiastes. Ecclesiasticus comes from the second century B.C.

ELOHIM, ELOHISTIC—The Hebrew word for "deity" is 'Elohim, as distinct from the personal name of the God of Israel, Yahweh.

ESCHATOLOGY, ESCHATOLOGICAL—Terms referring to "the last things," the consummation of the historical drama in the purpose of God.

EXILE (preexilic, postexilic)—One of the decisive events in Israel's history was the destruction of Jerusalem by the Babylonians in 587 B.C. and the deportation of major elements of the population into exile in Babylonia (modern Iraq). The edict of the Persian king, Cyrus, permitted Jewish exiles to return to their homeland (538 B.C. and after).

EXISTENTIAL, EXISTENTIALLY—These words refer to the life of the existing individual; the opposite is a detached view of existence, as though one were a spectator. For the existing individual death is an existential concern, whereas insurance companies (with their actuarial tables) take a detached view.

FORM CRITICISM—An approach to the Bible which interprets units of literature in terms of their literary form or type (genre) and understands these units in the context of their situation in life.

GENRE—A kind, sort or species. In this study the word refers to a literary type (e.g., hymn, lament, thanksgiving) which has a clear form (compare the sonnet).

HALLELUJAH—A Hebrew exclamation of praise—literally, "Praise Yahweh."

HELLENISTIC—Referring to the postclassical ancient Greek period of culture, after the time of Alexander the Great (336-323 B.C.).

HITTITES—In the middle of a second millennium B.C. this people established a powerful empire in Asia Minor (modern Turkey) which reached into Palestine and eventually came into conflict with Egypt.

HYMNODY (HYMNIC)—The singing or composition of sacred songs or hymns.

ICONOCLASTIC—Destroying religious images; attacking cherished beliefs as based on superstition.

IMPRECATION—A curse or malediction. In the ancient world, as in some societies today, a word spoken in curse (damnation) was held to be laden with terrific power.

ISRAEL—An ancient name for the People of God, bound together on the basis of common worship and legal responsibility. Although the term came to be applied to the nation, especially the Northern Kingdom, it always retained its basic religious meaning of the community which God called into being.

KI—The Hebrew word *ki* ("for," "because") often occupies a "key" position (to resort to an English pun) in a literary form. For instance, it may be the word to introduce a passage which gives the motive for praise.

LIBATION—The pouring out of wine or other liquid on the ground or altar as an act of sacrifice in honor of a deity.

LITURGY, LITURGICAL—Words referring to public service of worship and especially to the forms used in such service.

MACCABEAN—An adjective referring to the revival of the Jewish state under the leadership of the family of the Maccabees. The period began with the Maccabean revolt of 168 B.C. and ended with the arrival of the Roman general, Pompei, in 63 B.C.

MESSIAH—The Hebrew term *mashiah* (corresponding to Greek *christos*) refers to the Anointed One, chiefly the king who was anointed for office. It came to refer to *the* King who would come to inaugurate God's rule.

METAPHOR—A figure of speech in which one thing is likened to another as if it were that other, e.g., "All the world's a stage."

MILLENNIUM—One thousand years.

MYTH—Today myth often refers to a body of images and symbols by which a people traditionally portray the human situation. It also refers to a story of the gods which in ancient pagan religions was reenacted and actualized in the cult with the conviction that what happened in the beginning set the pattern for man's existence.

NUMINOUS—A sense of the holy.

ORACLE—A communication from God.

PATRISTIC—Of or pertaining to the fathers of the Christian Church or their writings.

PIETISM—Today the word often refers to an excessive emphasis upon feeling or emotion. (A movement inaugurated during the latter part of the 17th century for the revival and advancement of piety in the Lutheran churches in Germany.)

POLYTHEISM—The view that man's life is subject to the influence and control of many gods. In the second milennium B.C. polytheistic religions, such as the Canaanite, conceived of the deities as organized in a hierarchy or pantheon, with the supreme god and goddess at the top.

PRINCIPALITIES—The orders of "angels" or heavenly powers.

PROTOTYPE—An original model, of which later versions are copies. The word approximates the meaning of "archetype," though it often emphasizes the correspondence between "the first" and "the last" in a time sequence.

PSALTER—A title for the book of Psalms derived from the Greek word *psalterion*, referring to a song to the accompaniment of stringed instruments.

PSYCHOSOMATIC—A word composed of two elements, "soul, mind" and "body," used in this discussion to indicate the unity of man's being in contrast to the Greek view that man is a duality of "body" and "soul."

SALVATION HISTORY—The story of God's actions with his people which, in the Christian view, comes to climax and fulfillment in Jesus Christ. The corresponding term in German is *Heilsgeschichte* which contains the elements "history" (*Geschichte*) and "salvation" (*Heil*). Salvation refers to "health, healing, well-being, wholeness" which God wills for his people and which, through them, he bestows upon all mankind.

SEMITIC—Pertaining to Shem, the son of Noah; belonging to the racial grouping which includes Arabs, Jews, and related peoples.

SEPTUAGINT—The Greek translation of the Old Testament which was initiated in Alexandria, Egypt, about 250 B.C.

SHEOL—The Old Testament term for the realm of death and darkness ("hell"). According to the ancient pictorial way of thinking, it was situated in the subterranean waters of chaos.

SOUL—A frequent RSV translation (e.g., in Ps. 103) of the Hebrew word *nefesh*. This word, however, does not convey the Greek notion "soul" (a deathless spirit within the body); rather, it refers to the "self," the "person" as a psychosomatic (soul-body) unity.

STELE—An upright slab or pillar of stone bearing an inscription, sculptural design, or the like.

STROPHE—The first of two or more metrically corresponding series of lines forming divisions of a lyric poem, or in a longer poem, the first section of such a metrical pattern whenever it is repeated.

SUMERIANS—In the third millennium B.C. this people created a brilliant culture in Mesopotamia whose major center was Ur—the traditional city of Abraham.

SYNAGOGUE—This word refers to an assembly or gathering together for the purpose of prayer and scriptural interpretation. The synagogue emerged in the postexilic period and eventually came to be the major focus of Jewish community life.

THEOPHANY—A manifestation or appearance of deity to man.

TORAH—A Hebrew word meaning "instruction, direction, teaching." According to Israelite tradition the *torah* of Yahweh is given preeminently in the first five books of the Old Testament (Genesis through Deuteronomy), otherwise known as the Pentateuch.

TRANSCENDENT—In theology, going beyond the limits of human experience or knowledge; the opposite, *immanent*, refers to what is given in and understandable within human experience.

UGARITIC—An ancient Semitic language, closely related to Phoenician and Hebrew.

VICEGERENT—A deputy regent; one who acts in place of a ruler.

VOTIVE—Given by vow, or in fulfillment of a vow or promise, or in devotion.

VULGATE—The Latin version of the Scriptures, translated by Jerome (342-419 A.D.) and accepted as the authorized version by the Roman Catholic Church at the Council of Trent (A.D. 1545-63).

YAHWEH—The special, personal name of the God of Israel. Owing to the sacred nature of the Name, the Israelite people in the postexilic period adopted a substitute reading Adonai ("Lord"). This was translated as *kurios* ("Lord") in the Septuagint, following synagogue usage. The RSV has adopted this usage by translating "Yahweh" as "the Lord." The word "Jehovah," found in older English versions, is an artificial form composed of the consonants of Yahweh and the vowels of Adonai.

SUPPLEMENTARY MATERIALS *

OUT OF THE DEPTHS: The Psalms Speak to Us Today. *Study of the Psalms* by Bernhard W. Anderson. $1.25.

GUIDE, to "OUT OF THE DEPTHS" for *Leaders and Students of the Psalms*. George W. Frey. 75 cents.

WORSHIP WITH WORDS AND MOVEMENT. *For Psalms and other Scripture*. Doris Peterson. 60 cents.

THE PSALMS, *a special edition for this study* (RSV), 35 cents.

PSALMS '70. *A new approach to old prayers*. Mary Perkins Ryan. $2.75.

POSTER *on Psalms* (one of three in a mailing tube). $1.50.

I AM NO LONGER MY OWN . . . BUT THINE. John Wesley's Covenant Prayer. (prayer card) 5 cents; 25 for $1.00.

[1] FIFTY PSALMS: An Attempt at a New Translation. Huub Oosterhuis, Michel van der Plas, and others. Herder & Herder. $3.95.

Other Materials

PRAYER CALENDAR: *Board of Missions, The United Methodist Church*. $1.00.

PRAY FOR WORLD LEADERS: *United Nations Prayer Card*. Free.

CEREMONIES, RITES, AND SERVICES (new edition). $1.00.

FLORENCE ALLSHORN, ed. by J. H. Oldham. $1.75.

DIMENSIONS OF PRAYER. Douglas V. Steere. $1.00.

THAT THE WORLD MAY BELIEVE. Albert C. Outler. $1.00.

COMING TO LIFE: A Study of the Gospel of John. Ernest W. Saunders. $1.25.

* ORDER FROM Service Center, Board of Missions, The United Methodist Church, 7820 Reading Road, Cincinnati, Ohio 45237

[1] Order From Cokesbury Bookstore.

BIBLIOGRAPHY *

Ancient Near Eastern Texts Relating to the Old Testament, 3rd ed., ed. by J. B. Pritchard (Princeton: Princeton University Press, 1969).

A standard reference work containing texts that bear on the Old Testament, brought to light by archaeological research.

Anderson, Bernhard W., *Understanding the Old Testament,* 2nd ed. (Englewood Cliffs, N.J.: Prentice-Hall, 1966).

See the discussion of the growth of the Psalter, p. 82 ff.

Anderson, Bernhard W., *Creation versus Chaos* (New York: Association Press, 1967).

See especially chapter 3, "Creation and Worship."

Barth, Christoph, *Introduction to the Psalms,* Scribner Studies in Biblical Interpretation (New York: Chas. Scribner's Sons, 1966).

An excellent introduction, especially illuminating on theological issues.

Bright, John, *A History of Israel* (Philadelphia: The Westminster Press, 1959).

A standard work which should be studied alongside the work by Martin Noth listed below.

Clements, R. E., *God and Temple* (Philadelphia: Fortress Press, 1969).

A valuable study of the Jerusalem temple as the center of Yahweh's presence.

* Order From Cokesbury Bookstore.

Dahood, Mitchell, *The Psalms*, 2 vols.: Vol. 16 and Vol. 17, Anchor Bible Series (New York: Doubleday and Co., 1966 and 1968.)

A thorough work, somewhat technical in character.

Drijvers, Pius, *The Psalms: Their Structure and Meaning* (New York: Herder and Herder, 1964). (out of print)

A clear, concise introduction by a Roman Catholic scholar, who uses a form-critical approach.

Eichrodt, Walther, *Theology of the Old Testament*, I, trans. by J. A. Baker from the 6th German edition (Philadelphia: Westminster, 1961); II (1967).

A monumental work, one of the best theological works of our time, to be compared with the work by Gerhard von Rad (see below).

Gunkel, Hermann, *The Psalms: A Form-Critical Introduction*, with an introduction by James Muilenburg, Facet Books, Biblical Series, 19 (Philadelphia: Fortress Press, 1967).

An important essay by the brilliant pioneer of the form-critical study of the Psalms.

Guthrie, Harvey H., *Israel's Sacred Songs: A Study of Dominant Themes* (New York: Seabury Press, 1966).

As the title indicates, this book approaches the psalms by studying major themes.

Harrelson, Walter J., *Interpreting the Old Testament* (New York: Holt, Rinehart and Winston, 1964).

A helpful commentary on the Old Testament which follows essentially a book-by-book approach.

The Interpreter's Dictionary of the Bible, 4 vols., ed. by

G. A. Buttrick and others (New York: Abingdon, 1962). One of the best Bible dictionaries available.

Jerome Biblical Commentary, ed. by R. E. Brown, J. A. Fitzmeyer, and R. E. Murphy (Englewood Cliffs, N.J.: Prentice-Hall, 1969).

An excellent one-volume commentary by Roman Catholic scholars.

The Jerusalem Bible, ed. by Alexander Jones (New York: Doubleday and Co., 1966).

Annotated biblical text with brief introductory essays, produced by Roman Catholic scholars. A good companion to the *Oxford Annotated Bible* (see below).

Kraus, Hans-Joachim, *Worship in Israel: A Cultic History of the Old Testament*, trans. by Geoffrey Buswell (Oxford: Basil Blackwell; Richmond, Va.: John Knox Press, 1966).

A fresh and illuminating outline of the history of Israel's worship.

Leslie, Elmer A., *The Psalms: Translated and Interpreted in the Light of Hebrew Life and Worship* (New York: Abingdon Press, 1968).

The influence of Gunkel is evident in this commentary.

Mowinckel, Sigmund, *The Psalms in Israel's Worship*, *I-II* (New York: Abingdon Press, 1963).

Here another great pioneer in Psalm research has illumined the Psalms in the light of ancient Near Eastern religious practice.

Noth, Martin, *The History of Israel*, 2nd ed., trans. by

Stanley Godman and revised by P. R. Ackroyd (New York: Harper and Row, 1960).

One of the major works in the field, to be compared with the work by John Bright cited above.

Oxford Annotated Bible with the Apocrypha, ed. by H. G. May and B. M. Metzger (New York: Oxford University Press, 1962).

This important study-tool is based on the Revised Standard Version and is provided with articles, notes, maps, and other aids.

Paterson, John, *The Praises of Israel* (New York: Chas. Scribner's Sons, 1950). Out of print.

A sensitive study by a scholar who understands the Psalter from within.

Rhodes, A. B., *The Psalms*, The Layman's Bible Commentary (Richmond, Va.: John Knox Press, 1960).

Ringgren, Helmer, *The Faith of the Psalmists* (Philadelphia: Fortress Press, 1963).

A first-rate study which illumines the piety of the Psalms in the light of the cultic situation emphasized particularly by Scandinavian scholars.

Rowley, H. H., *Worship in Ancient Israel: Its Forms and Meaning* (London: S.P.C.K., 1967; Philadelphia: Fortress Press).

A study which illuminates the cultic situation of the psalms, by the late dean of British Old Testament scholars.

Terrien, Samuel, *The Psalms and Their Meaning for Today* (Indianapolis: Bobbs-Merrill, 1952).

A clearly written, theologically penetrating study.

A Theological Wordbook of the Bible, ed. by Alan Richardson (New York: The Macmillan Co., 1951).

A concise, useful dictionary of theological terms.

Von Rad, Gerhard, *Old Testament Theology*, I-II, trans. by D. M. G. Stalker (New York: Harper and Row, 1962, 1966).

A fresh and incisive study of Israel's "salvation history." A work to be compared with that of Walther Eichrodt, listed above.

Weiser, Artur, *The Psalms: A Commentary*, trans. by Herbert Hartwell, Old Testament Library (Philadelphia: Westminster Press, 1962).

The best commentary available in English at this time.

Westermann, Claus, *The Praise of God in the Psalms*, 2nd ed., trans. by Keith R. Crim (Richmond, Va.: John Knox Press, 1965).

One of the most important form-critical studies of the Psalter since Hermann Gunkel.

THE AUTHOR

This restudy of the Book of Psalms, OUT OF THE DEPTHS, is undertaken in the conviction that the Psalms are actually "the prayer book of the church" which is as timely for the People of God today as in the past. In a revolutionary age, when overwhelming and earth-shaking problems confront men, often leading them to cry "out of the depths," the laments, thanksgivings, and hymns found in the Psalter speak to where we are living.

Dr. Bernhard W. Anderson is also the author of other books on the Bible, including *Rediscovering the Bible; The Unfolding Drama of the Bible; The Beginning of History; Understanding the Old Testament,* and *Creation versus Chaos.* He is editor of *The Old Testament and Christian Faith,* co-editor of *Israel's Prophetic Heritage,* and the translator and contributor to Martin Noth's *A History of Pentateuchal Traditions.*

Professor of Old Testament Theology at Princeton Theological Seminary, Dr. Anderson, before coming to Princeton, was the Henry Anson Buttz Professor of Biblical Theology, Drew University, and for nine years served as Dean of the Theological School. Before that he held positions at Colgate University, the University of North Carolina, and the Colgate Rochester Divinity School. His teaching career has been devoted to interpreting the Scriptures in the context of contemporary life.

Born in Dover, Missouri, Dr. Anderson was educated in California where he received degrees from the College of the Pacific and Pacific School of Religion. In 1939 he was ordained to the ministry of The Methodist Church. He served Methodist churches in California, as well as Congregational churches in Connecticut and New York.

In 1945 he received the degree of Doctor of Philosophy at Yale University where he specialized in Old Testament studies. During the academic year 1963-64 he served as Annual Professor at the American School of Oriental Research in Jerusalem. He holds honorary degrees from the Pacific School of Religion, the University of the Pacific, and Colgate University.

In OUT OF THE DEPTHS Dr. Anderson, by approaching the Psalms in terms of their *forms* and *situations in life*, proposes how readers may identify with the language of the psalmists and may sense their involvement in "the unfolding drama" of God's dealings with his people in their ongoing historical pilgrimage.

NOTES

NOTES